Scrumptious Couples

ISBN: 0615599044
ISBN-13: 9780615599045
Sandpoint, Idaho
Library of Congress Control Number: 2012932395

Scrumptious Couples

Reconnecting, redefining, and strengthening
your most amazing partnership

Kestrel J Bass

To my beloved Tom

I wish to acknowledge my three children, Christen, Sara and Sam for their exorable courage, humor, love and support. My wonderful husband for his many contributions and gentle nudging's to this end, and all the truly remarkable souls I have met along this journey of learning, who have never once judged me and who have always been there to lift and support me, and who continue to do so.

"Stretch, intrepid dreamers!
Look into your dragon's eyes,
Grab on to his wings
And dare to soar above the clouds."

K . B .

Finding Our Way to Snowhawk

The weather forecast calls for more snow. Already we have twelve inches. Predictably, the wind is beginning to stir, and the fat, wet snowflakes are falling erratically to the ground. It seems damp outside, and the sky looks an almost sickly gray color.

Our tiny cabin stands alone in the frosty forest, her bonnet of green tin barely peeking out from beneath the mounds of snow piled upon it. With her icicle lights twinkling and Tom's collection of firewood stacked about her porch, she looks so sweet and inviting—to me, rather like a portly little grandma awaiting her grandkids with arms outstretched.

I've got a teapot on the stove stuffed with cloves, cinnamon sticks, and eucalyptus leaves. The delicate, little tree that Tom and I hauled from the overrun crush of fir trees behind the cabin is standing in the corner, near the fireplace, bedecked with garlands of dried cranberries and dotted with pinecones. I've saved a few special ornaments from Christmases long past, but most have been doled out to the kids for their own trees.

Our mantle is covered with bows of cedar and fir. Two silver candlesticks from my own mother's house stand sweetly among them. If Tom isn't watching the Weather Channel to see what storms are looming around the corner, he has the Christmas CDs playing at full blast. I swear he's forgotten where he hid the Christmas gifts from Jim and Gary that came last week. In his haste to hide them from my impatient hands, he's managed to misplace them himself. A truly remarkable feat if you consider we live in a matchbox of 583 square feet.

It is our first Christmas without the kids. Usually someone is with us, but this year they are all off on their own. I must say, though, Tom's been wonderful to put up with my gloomy disposition and sour attitude. At times, I find myself staring aimlessly at the little tree or out the window. If I wished and hoped well and hard enough, perhaps somehow the past would miraculously appear before me. I'm having trouble letting go. My brain says that life goes on, but my heart says, "Stop!"

However we find ourselves without kids and all that wonderful chaos that comes with them. Life has changed immeasurably. Some relationships can bear the change, while others find they now have little in common. With no one to tend to other than ourselves and our mates, who may have long been neglected for other priorities, it can be, for sure, a difficult transition.

It hasn't been such an easy life for either of us. Hopes and dreams bolted out the door all too early, grabbing trust and faith as they fled. Poor choices confounded any hope of a stable home life for years, and the children endured the uncertainty of divorces. But surprisingly, among the crippling fear and endless stress came gifts more unanticipated and more precious than any Christmas package could contain.

But life marches on, and its bounties still manage to be bestowed onto our front stoop. We welcome them always, but for me, I struggle sometimes with the idea that they may someday be snatched away, once again revealing life's erratic and oft times cruel temperament. Leftovers, I guess.

We had to go into town yesterday. Tom seems to take this weather in stride. He brags constantly how adept he is at driving in two feet of snow. I'd rather sit in the warm confines of this little cabin and wait for the groceries to come to me. A fair trade, I think, since I have been relegated to full-time cook. It is the consequence of living this unconventional lifestyle. It is not for everyone. Heavy work must be done this time of year to keep the driveway clear of snow and keep the wood piled on the cabin deck. There are also the mundane chores of housekeeping, cooking, and duck, chicken, and doggy-tending.

Speaking of which, it is an absolute conundrum to me that Dumbleduck and the gang, an assortment of chickens and ducks, haven't frozen to death thus far. I schlep out to the coop each morning with hot water for them, give them a handful of dog food (which they seem to prefer over cracked corn and poultry food), fluff up the straw, and leave. What a life! If I were a Buddhist, I'd rather think they weren't very compassionate in their previous incarnations to be some sort of fowl, stuck in North Idaho for the winter. Tom does say time and again that they have to be the most spoiled bunch in the state!

We drove into town again yesterday. Tom had an appointment, and so did I. I closed my eyes out of sheer fright for nine miles, which drove him nuts. The roads are icy and treacherous, with twists, bends, and no guardrails. I refuse to feel shamed. It is well within my rights to be timid and long-suffering if I see the need. I did!

I had made it pretty clear that if he wanted me to continue working, we needed to be somewhere with roads that were at least paved and preferably snowless. I know I was dismissed as just ranting about nothing. Once I was here, surely I would brave up and see the joys of driving in the muck of things, but sadly for both of us, I didn't…and I won't, and oh well!

Tom had to go to the dentist; an appointment he frets over for weeks before he has to be there. He whines and pouts and makes life horrible until it's over. Then, after Motrin and a couple of Black Butte porters, he settles back down a bit until the next go-round. And I'm the coward!

Because it was two degrees outside this morning, we had little choice but to leave the dogs in the cabin. This is not a good thing. All of them, George (the cat) included, have honed their thievery skills to near perfection. Over the years they have had plenty of practice. Marley, our older Golden, single-pawedly (is that a real word?) is able to open a package of goodies and remove and consume its contents without so much as leaving a morsel behind. He can also delicately eat the pie filling out of a glass pie plate and still keep it on the counter. I thought I was going mad!

He has scoped out cookies hiding in the drawers and sniffed out muffins in the breadbox. Murphy, our other sweet boy, also a Golden, is his compadre in crime, but

I am convinced if he was left alone he wouldn't have the nerve to do half the things Marley's done. George, we can assume, does his part as well by batting goodies off the counter onto the floor for all to partake in. Yum!

Frodo is our dachshund, a gift from our daughter (and yes, we seem to have gotten ourselves a bit of a menagerie). He is worse than any of them. He lives for food. The complete gall of this boy is remarkable. Telltale signs of foul play have given him up on more than one occasion too. He is the smallest and most shameless of the dogs, which therefore enables him to reach even higher realms of devastation. Just last night, in fact, Tom caught him rummaging inside the lower kitchen cabinet. I believe I was cooking at the time.

Frodo has also developed a propensity for disemboweling anything with stuffing so as to get at the squeaky thing inside. We learned early on, in Newport, Rhode Island, when we were stationed at the War College, that if we came home from work and there was no happy, bouncing puppy (we only had Marley at the time) at the door, it meant one less loaf of bread or box of cookies, or garbage strewn all over. Marley even managed, at one point, to unwrap candy kisses and eat only the chocolate. How is that even possible?

Anyway, such was the case when we returned from town. The stillness was chilling. None of them even budged from their beds. All looked painfully guilty of something. Purposely, I left the stringing of the popcorn for after the trip. Purposely, I put all the goodies on the top shelf and closed the breadbox. Foolishly, I left the ornaments on the tree! Gradually we noticed fluff, bits of red felt, paper, and tinsel under the coffee table and next to the tree. My favorite ornaments—destroyed! Chewed beyond recognition! Shame on them all…so out they all went into the blistering cold without the slightest remorse on my part.

But today dawns brightly and all is forgiven…not that they stayed out more than five minutes anyway. Once again, the snow is falling, but the sky seems kinder and more alive. It is my birthday. A day I wish to forget, but am reminded of with each well-wishing phone call. I am also incessantly reminded, with each passing year, of my physical downward spiral. Everything on my body seems to be heading in the wrong direction. There is no stopping this train. All I can think about is the line in *The Wizard of Oz*: "I'm melting! I'm melting!"

For my special day, Tom sometimes gifts me a spa day. It's a day he somewhat reluctantly agrees to give me, but after all, today is my birthday! It means dusting off the massage table, a facial, painted toenails, and whatever else I deem absolutely essential to make me feel beautiful and sexy. Ego be damned!

I have come to accept Tom's inability to shop for anything other than food. I have learned that instead of being upset by the choice of gifts gotten at Safeway the night before an occasion, I would rather just announce what I want and get on with it. Believe me, I fought this tooth and nail for years, getting myself in a lather time and again, feeling unappreciated and miserable. But truly, he is just challenged in this area; he really doesn't get it. I don't take it personally anymore, because he does so much for me day in and day out. I have learned to live with this particular flaw, and in all honesty, it has worked out in my favor.

So inconceivably delightful, in fact, is this gift of a spa day to me that I have delayed the inevitable, hoping to let it continue into the wee hours of the evening. Fortunately for my wonderful, if still a bit unenlightened husband, this year I've mislaid my nail polish, so there is one less tortuous task for him to perform. Nevertheless, I have bottles of bubbles, exfoliating cream somewhere in the drawer, that sturdy massage table, oils, and an old bottle of Bailey's I've had hidden for months. All is good!

The fire is crackling downstairs, and Tom is outside blowing snow from the driveway with his beloved (yes, that's the right word) John Deer snow blower. The plume rises twenty feet into the air, landing not only on the banks lining the driveway, but on Tom as well. He has to drive the thing backwards up the driveway to clear the road. This seems outrageous to me, because he usually emerges from these expeditions standing on the porch with a full grin peeking out from a frozen and snow-laden face. His mountain-man hat, with its floppy ears at right angles from his neck, is usually topped with about three extra inches of snow, and his beard has, in one hour, usually grown longer and become festooned with silvery gray icicles. My delight!

Each day we try to take our daily trek to the mailbox, the dogs in tow, of course, bounding and plowing through the great depths of snow, Frodo boinking about with ears flopping and tail wagging, barely able to stay in our tracks. We usually wade through the back woods, now almost knee-deep in snow, to get to the road. It is a picture-perfect postcard, almost more beautiful in the winter months than any other time of year. Snow has a camouflaging effect on nasty, stumpy trees and dilapidated yards; it envelops the land with such beauty as to take our breath away.

Along the trail we are like children: throwing snowballs at each other and the dogs, tripping over hidden brush, and on that rare occasion falling face first into the frozen beauty of it all. What fun it is—although I can't help longing for the times the kids will all be here with us. It is for them that we built Snowhawk.

It has been an interesting journey to her door. As we were becoming entrenched in the process of moving, we were both very much aware of the synchronistic way in which we were led to Northern Idaho.

Our home in Langley, Washington, had been dubbed "the heart of the neighborhood." It was a house designed from a woodshed blueprint I found at the hardware store. There was a sweetness to it with its little veggie garden in front and odd little doodads here and there about the property. It looked over the ocean with a spectacular view of Mt. Baker. My ex-husband and I built it, and Tom and I spent five years finishing it. I think we all put a little of our souls into that lovely home.

It had become an intrinsic and beloved part of both of us, but the island, once a sleepy, mellow sanctuary, was now becoming littered with new, fancy homes that had equally fancy price tags. With the kids mostly gone and one still in limbo, the encroachment of too many people and our new sense of freedom, we began the deliberate and daunting process of uprooting from a place that had once felt so safe and comfortable. It was time to leave the island and look for a home where there was space to move and new adventures to be had.

Regrettably, it meant giving up the close proximity we had enjoyed to family and friends, but we also foresaw our kids going in their own directions, not to mention our take on the uncertainty of world dynamics.

Change is seldom easy. It carries much baggage, sometimes plenty of heartache and fear, but usually also the promise and excitement of a new beginning. It was all these things and much more for us.

I remember walking down the long driveway here at Snowhawk for the first time and thinking to myself that this may be it. The property had been removed from the real estate market only recently due to few if any lookers. Its owners were in another part of the state, and it seemed a tired piece of land, misused, abused, and all but abandoned. Our agent showed it to us on a whim because he happened to live nearby. There was no well, no power; it was way, way off the beaten path and had a crummy, unlivable little cabin not fit for the mice living in it. But Tom and I felt a spark anyway. It had lots of land, a somewhat well-built but unfinished barn, about two acres of cleared space, and best of all, it had a beautiful little pond. Just right!

It was one of those heart decisions that perhaps was not as well thought out as it should have been. We had no idea what we were doing, no idea how to even start to fix this little sad part of the earth, and certainly no idea how expensive it would all be. Country living isn't cheap!

Upon mentioning to the locals where we were going to move, a most peculiar grin would start forming on their faces. Their eyes would roll around in their sockets, and they usually let out some kind of indistinct sound. Much to our horror, this didn't happen on just one or two occasions, but each and every time we puffed out our chests with pride to tell others of our newly found gem.

From these gestures we cleverly deduced that perhaps we may have been a bit hasty and lacked some clear judgment concerning the location of our new little love nest. But no matter—we have come to believe it is as it should be. Whether we have made a colossal mistake or a very good decision is yet to be known.

Of course, although we were told the cabin would be finished by May, it wasn't. It was barely started by then, so we found ourselves stuffed into our not-so-comfy barn. At least it wasn't cold yet. We had our grill for cooking, and sleeping bags and lawn chairs. The one inconvenience was really the lack of warm water. The pond, after all, is spring-fed. Thank goodness it was temporary.

We bulldozed the existing cabin and built a new one. We mended and tore down fences and pulled out stumps, and Tom rolled up endless feet of barbed wire. We cleaned up enormous piles of brush strewn senselessly all over the place. We put up an eight-foot deer fence around the garden space, which had been used to corral some horses and was perfect. We were ready for next spring!

Snowhawk slowly shed her rough exterior to expose a soft and gentle underbelly. She was starting to heal herself.

I must say it was fun to watch the cabin grow. I think the best part was watching the river-rock chimney being made. It is enormous and absolutely beautiful. The gentleman who built it, Al, is a master stone builder. There was no shortage of stones either. Tom and I gathered them from all over the land and then hauled them all to the cabin. Al hoisted them all up on the scaffolding and artistically placed each one in its perfect spot.

Al built us stone steps up to the cabin too. When he was almost done, Tom placed special stones, each etched with a picture of a Golden Retriever, on either side of the steps, one for each of our beloved companions. I am so grateful that he did too.

Even the stone hearth in the kitchen has special stones in it. One is even heart shaped. We also had our grandkids put their handprints in a cement tablet that Al then set right in the middle of our fireplace. It's perfect.

Our cabin is 583 square feet. We went from a 2,300 square-foot house on the edge of the ocean to a tiny cabin at the edge of a vast national forest. As soon as we could, we stuffed our furniture into the cabin and made our nest for the winter. It was absolutely delightful! Now came the hard part: how to cohabitate in such tight quarters, with only one bathroom? Hmm...

So this was winter in Idaho. Tom happily plowed through piles of snow on Gimili, our tractor named for the tough old dwarf in Tolkien's tall tale. He chopped wood, wrote, and generally took some well-earned time for himself. Besides my knitting, spinning, and endless hours on the computer, I had a myriad of other projects to keep me occupied for millennia.

We are having an adventure. We have decided to try and live as we have both talked of and written about so often. It is the beginning of a simpler way of life, engaging with the earth as much as we are able.

As we took a walk through the woods the other morning, the enchanted beauty before us wove a mystical path. The snowfall, which had ended only moments earlier, left the tree branches heavy and bent down to us, as if we were royalty inspecting a magical kingdom. A dowry of glistening diamonds was strewn at our feet, leading us deeper and deeper into secret places within the forest.

The cold of the air felt clean and sweet on our faces, and the silence of Spirit seemed to wrap a blanket of warmth all around us as we waded through the powdery winter snow back to our little home. It is during these few, special moments that I find my heart allows a tiny opening. For an instant, I manage to touch a place where my soft beauty dances, in tune with the image I see each morning reflected back to me in my bathroom mirror. The old cedar tree standing watch over our north pasture is my father. The boulders, with their funny white caps almost immersed in the cold river water, are brothers; the moose that lumbers occasionally across our frozen pound, my uncle.

All are connected. All are one. But all at once I am distracted by even the slightest soft chirp of a snowbird or the crunch of ice crystals under my boot. I am back to forgetting about such things and am concerning myself with the dinner menu. About the only thing left to me is the knowing of what could be if I simply trusted and allowed what is. For now, for me, this is enough.

Our time here will bring forth many stories and help us to grow in ways we never thought of before. It is a time of life when stillness can offer us an abundant basket of comfort. Every stage of life brings with it such richness. At Snowhawk, we are hoping to tap into that abundance, reach for that appreciation, and feel the wholeness of who we both truly are.

Tom is up and out already. We have a routine now, which I suppose we have always had, although now it's just whenever we want. I make the coffee and the fire, now that we have a wood-burning stove, and he gets dressed and ready to work outside. Usually, in the darkness of the winter months there is new-fallen snow to be plowed off the drive before we can venture out. This means the fuss and bother of putting on layer after layer of old shirts and sweaters, his old motorcycle "snowsuit," as I call it, his sheepskin floppy-eared hat again, "glubs" (so called thanks to one of the kids) two sets of socks, long underwear and his boots. It's a painful process to watch, but eventually he is ready to trudge outside.

In the chill of the season, once he is outside, I will confess to sometimes crawling back into bed and squirming deep under the covers to hurry the time along. But since the days are light earlier now, I am more inclined to stay up and start my day.

It isn't long before one of the dogs is whimpering to go out, anyway. Our cat, George, which we all know to be a little boy in a cat suit, is scratching at one of our loft posts, goading me to throw a pillow at him in protest. This little irritation is also a morning routine, one that even on a Saturday, regrettably, seems to go on. I suppose if we had a larger home we could confine them all to some remote room on the other side of the house, but since our cabin is at best twenty by twenty, with at least eight posts up in the loft sufficient for a good scratch, we suffer each other's company at this time of day.

As the winter months melt into spring's newness, the sun's rays reflect off the needles of the tallest trees atop Mt. Pend Oreille, just to the east of us, and our little pond begins to stretch with the life it has doggedly held all the winter long.

In the light of the morning, a fine coating of minuscule insects hover a fraction of an inch above the water's surface. It seems only noticeable in the early hours of the morning, although I would guess that it lingers there most of the day, regardless of the light. The fish feed well, filling their long-empty bellies, and splashing in the celebration of the freedom they feel from their wintry bonds of ice and cold. It is May, and we have made it through our first Idaho winter!

The Pine Siskins, Black Capped Chickadees, and Nuthatches are beginning to gather more wildly at the feeders now, and the Barn Swallows are here to start their families and feed on the bugs that the pond generates. Since bear is just now starting to wake, we are cautious about how much feed we put in the feeders, and watch carefully that the dogs don't venture too far from home.

Last spring when we were at the very beginning of building the cabin, I happily, but ignorantly, stuck our lovely, tall bird feeder down into the marsh near the cabin. It was one of the first gifts Tom ever gave me, and I cherished it. I suppose people just automatically assume you know what you're doing around here...but well, not us. No one told us not to put out birdseed when the bears were still wandering about. At any rate, I filled my birdfeeder with lots of goodies and was done with it.

Not long after that little chore was completed, Tom caught me running full-bore into the cabin when a black bear snuck up behind me and gorged himself on the feeder and its contents. Thank goodness, he was little concerned with me. I can laugh now!

Bear can be very quiet if it pleases him, which it most always does. They will shamelessly demolish anything with food in it and even go so far as to unscrew the tops of hummer bottles and gulp down the juice. Our neighbor seems to have particular trouble with them. It seems the critters have taken a particular liking to his sunny deck, and if they're lucky, he's forgotten about the juice and they get a free snack with accommodations.

The road to Snowhawk has not been without its sleepless nights. Although Tom and I felt a draw to this area and a fullness of Spirit here, it was going to be an unconventional lifestyle that neither of us had experienced before. Needless to say, we were a bit anxious. The choice was made with a knowing and a belief that we needed to be here. The path here was mostly effortless, but still the real and true purpose had not been revealed to us, and there was a good chance it never would be. I suppose we felt we were compelled to take a huge leap of faith.

It is a part of a belief system not all embrace, but one we individually and collectively have come to appreciate and stand in awe of. We have learned to listen inside and follow those feelings, at least as much as we are able. We are deeply grateful for this adventure and the ability to have it. We are learning so much about so many things. Not the least is a deep appreciation for every second of each day.

Over the years we hope our hearts have opened a bit wider and our minds have become clearer to the possibilities and the simple truth that all we need do is allow the love of ourselves, of each other, and of the greatness and wholeness of everything to carry us along a wave to unimaginable joy. Slowly we are getting a better understanding of the meaning behind that love, and therefore the magnitude of the power we all have within us to turn our human existence from one of complacency and tolerance into one of remarkable beauty and incredible wealth of Spirit.

Because of a ridiculous set of circumstances lumped together, we met and married in 1994. As with so many things in life, had one part of that dance not worked, the journey for us, together, wouldn't have begun at all.

There are two strong, healthy cedar trees on the south end of our property that have grown together at their bases. We have noticed that cedar trees often do this. Each has very distinctive and strong limbs, but even so, they are joined forever, having established a common and sturdy foundation. So we began down a road together that, as individuals, made us better people, but together made us happier, more grounded, and more whole than ever before.

I wish I could say we were young and unencumbered when we first met, but as it was, we were neither. Both had been through marriages, and both of us still had young children. But tagging along with all of this came a bit more wisdom, lots more appreciation, and a stronger commitment from each of us to make this relationship work and work well.

So we don't approach this book stuffed with the latest research and data on relationships. Rather we offer a few of our own suggestions for a thriving relationship that come from lives trapped, all too often, by life's quirky little erratic habits and seductive lures, and tossed about because of a myriad of other issues.

We've both seen delightfully good times, as well as horribly bad times. Sadly, our kids have endured our bad choices and situations along with us. But happily, they have also been recipients of the love and laughter that we eventually found in each other and ourselves.

Unfortunately, we seem to get our best growth spurts from making mistakes. Our children have seen what two people do to each other in a bad relationship, as well as how good they can be together in a remarkable one.

People are all different, and their approaches to life and love are all varied. One person doesn't make a relationship. A beautiful, scrumptious relationship takes two dedicated, selfless, kind, and accepting people. To be accepted for who we are is a most precious gift. When it comes from our best friend and lover, no gift is worth more.

We gift this little bit of us to our children and grandchildren, that they may know a little more about who we are and what we have come to learn on this wondrous pathway to never-ending awareness and love.

For those who opt to reconnect to their more passionate beginnings, or for couples who have seen life at its worst and who feel beaten and weary but who may now, after retirement or after the kids have left, feel the life force begin to flow once more, we offer this little bit of us.

Our bumbling and stumbling through our own relationships may help in some small way to shed a bit more light on some piece of your own lives together.

It takes a big effort on everyone's part to bring a relationship back into focus. It requires no less effort to start up a new relationship after an old one has fizzled, or for that matter, to just keep a lovely ongoing relationship glowing brightly.

When we commit to making our relationship the most amazing it can be, then we'll most certainly be successful. Every book we read will help us through this process. Somewhere along the way, little words, phrases, and ideas will settle in to help. Be patient, consistent, and willing to grow. Help each other to understand your differences; don't merely set about trying to change them.

We are each incredible, individual souls with many, many love songs to sing. When we understand how precious each of us is and how much we are loved for just being, then maybe we will start to get the full meaning of life here on this amazing planet. Maybe then we can learn to forgive and get on with things, love and be loved, accept without judgment, and live as we are meant to live.

Thank you my dear one
You came, and you did
Well to come: I needed you
You have made
Love blaze up in
My breast—bless you!
Bless you often.
As hours have
Been endless to me
While you were gone.

S A P P H O

"Love, Commitment & Those Not-So-Easy Choices

ight from the start, we make choices. As we begin this life journey, they are recognized and accepted as reactive to our immediate needs. Little to no attention is paid to anyone other than ourselves. It isn't until we mature and become less self-involved that we take a more careful and methodical approach to choice making. We look a bit farther down the road to the consequences of our actions.

Some choices seem so benign and inconsequential that they appear to hardly warrant attention or thought at all. But even such innocuous choices like what to eat for breakfast, what color clothes to wear, who to call, or who to simply smile at on the street, can make a world of difference to more people than we think.

I have, on many occasions, been guilty of blissfully moving through my day unaware of the ripple effect my choices may have stirred up. All it takes is a bit of effort to become more consciously aware of our behavior. The idea of making good and careful choices is not news. But I don't suspect too many of us really quite have a clue as to how the tiniest of choices impacts others.

Many of us are aware of the larger choices that loom over us, not to mention the more dubious ones we've tucked neatly or not so neatly away in some corner of our minds. In hindsight, I've made some doozies. I look back with abject horror at a few of them. I want to deny making them and hide from the humiliation of them. I regret a multitude of rotten decisions but, sadly, I have had to live with the wretched consequences more times than I would like to admit. But, as we all ultimately must do at some point, I hope that I've grown and learned from all of them.

Sometimes, on those days that stir up the part of me that is determined to play up the mistakes I've made in my life, I try to opt instead to take a long, earnest look at the choices that have positively impacted my life and my family's lives. Many people have been shaped by the consequences of my choices and, concurrently, their choices have impacted me.

Each of us is connected, more tightly than we know, to the other through many astonishing ways. When we simply even smile at a stranger during the course of the day, or choose to be courteous rather than rude to the person stuck holding the "slow" traffic sign in frigid or sweltering weather, we just may have made a profound impact on that person's day. In turn, his or her reaction may impact another, and so on. By merely asking if we can be of some help to someone who looks to be in need, we may just have avoided an embarrassment to him or her. We don't know what may have been, only what is at that very moment. Ultimately, in positive ways, our affirming choices rebound to us too.

Changing choices is always possible. Listening inside to what could make a difference in our relationships and choosing to modify our behavior in a kind and generous way may eventually bring happiness and contentment to an otherwise gloomy situation. Ego has little room in a good relationship.

My husband and I chose to get rid of our mortgage and all our debt. Consequently, we had to give up a large home for a tiny cabin. We chose a new way of living for the experience of it. We gave up some things to gain others.

We rarely go out to dinner, opting to stay home together and enjoy a good bowl of homemade soup and bread. For entertainment, we play games or simply watch as nature whisks us away with its gripping beauty. We chose this way of life, as others would choose a bigger house and more frequent flyer miles. Each of us was meant to be happy and content, not miserable and stuck on an endless merry-go-round of poor choices and their consequences.

Sacrificing one's own happiness for another, time and time again, is not the right thing to do either. Both of you doing the very best within your relationship is what you committed to in the beginning. One person cannot hold the fortress up alone. It will ultimately create very unhappy, resentful feelings. Recognize what stones lay in your path. Take responsibility for clearing them away, and allow the other to walk on through. Life is a truly bountiful garden, but it takes much tending to have one that will take your breath away.

It is December now. The holiday season always seems to bring out the very best in most of us, although, sadly for some, it is a difficult reminder of hard times. We are remarkable and resilient people, full with the richness of our true souls, just waiting to shed the heavy burdens of life and scatter the seeds of our love and commitment to each other. It just sounds so much easier than it is.

I've come to believe that if we choose to listen inside, often the answers come more easily. The path spreads out a bit more gently before us. Doors open, and our souls are more content to continue on. As difficult as it may be at times to welcome the stillness of our own hearts, the choice to do so will most likely be a gratifying one.

Tom has a wonderful analogy for love. He says it's the house most of us want to build, and where most of us want and need to live. He calls the foundation of the house the strength of our commitment to our partner and the love that binds us together. But no house, be it cabin or mansion, is exempt from decay. Not every day dawns bright and sunny, full with hope and promise. Some days are gray, cold, and downright dreary. It isn't easy to love another; it takes a profound understanding of what it means to commit, as well as a love that's resolute enough to carry out such a promise of devotion. There's no other way in which to nourish a lifelong relationship, while at the same time thriving and growing as individuals.

Lots of us fall in love, but many find it a complicated and convoluted force of nature to deal with as we meander along life's bumpy path. New love, like the arrival of spring, is full with life, warmth and bustling with possibilities. The magick formula that brings two hearts together is, forever, one of life's most precious and mystifying gifts.

At the outset, we surrender rational thought to the intensity of a new love, but it's unrealistic to think we can sustain this same kind of powerful, euphoric feeling throughout our entire relationship. Sooner or later, just as the snows of winter follow fall, difficult times are an unavoidable part of the seasons of love.

My daughter Sara, who, when she was twenty-six, said she'd been though the relationship "meat grinder," as she called it, seemed unwilling to commit to men she deemed imperfect. Now, at the ripe old age of thirty, she has thankfully lowered her expectations. I am happy to report that they are a bit more realistic. Her dream man is no longer unattainable, but has decidedly human characteristics.

Things do change. Obviously, everyone has flaws, and, as my sister said to me so many years ago, "Finding the imperfections we can live with is the trick." So very wise!

Expecting that the initial excitement and lust we feel can sustain itself over time is, although possible, sadly more likely a fantasy. But over the years, a well-nourished relationship can eventually flourish into something even more spectacular, albeit a bit less fiery. The friendship and love we hold so dearly will be what sustains us in our relationships as time meanders by.

It's the wise couple that recognizes the need for shared dreams and goals. A lasting partnership that's positive, affirming, appreciative, and loving isn't out of reach for any of us; it's just closer to those willing to admit that a great couple doesn't just happen. It takes hard work and allegiance to one another. There can always be new creations, so begin at the beginning and make sure to build on firm, steady ground.

Our grandson unknowingly offered up a simple and fitting illustration for the value of a good foundation. A number of Thanksgivings ago, Jake, who was five at the time, was building a tall Lego tower. Unfortunately, it toppled over repeatedly, refusing to support the weight of all his mismatched pieces. He tried all sort of ways to make it stronger, but nothing worked for him. Finally he decided he needed to go back and spend some additional time redoing the foundation. So after much frustration, he finally had it standing in the corner of his room, amid a sea of jets, trucks, and other bits and pieces of valued things. It lasted a good long time too!

We can't overemphasize the importance of a sturdy, tough foundation in maintaining a healthy, thriving relationship that can sustain itself throughout all of life's inevitable blunders and misfortunes.

The commitment that upholds the foundation of love is nothing more than a promise: a promise to create a sage and healthy space in which to bloom; clearly, yet another, tricky, slippery slope—not for the fainthearted, but one that ultimately promises unimaginable rewards.

The challenges that are an inevitable part of family life all too often become tedious battles full of stress and disappointment. But, as devastating as a catastrophic illness rips at the heart of a family can be, so too can the daily grind of maintaining a household. It can wear thin the frayed fabric of a relationship.

Somewhere under the mounds of laundry, we're apt to lose sight of the very thing that attracted us in the beginning. The feeling that we're so cherished and revered can evaporate. In its place can be that empty, lonely, "What am I doing here?" feeling. It's easy to forget or ignore a promise in the middle of such a relentless siege.

The love, romance, and great sex that we once thought effortless, sadly, now take effort.

The road to Easy Street
goes right through the sewer.
– JOHN MADDEN

To me, it seems that avoiding effort is the great American pastime. Disposability is the name of the game. If it doesn't work, throw it out, trade it in, but, never, never put the time into fixing it. Get a new one, one that will work better for now, and, allegedly, make us feel better.. for now.

We're not just talking about a hairdryer or a toaster; we're referring to our unsatisfactory and underachieving partners. Seldom does the breakup of a relationship dispose of the real reasons things ultimately failed in the first place, but, for the moment, anyway, we've escaped.

Perhaps it's just too tough to see and accept responsibility, both in terms of making things work and being accountable for our part in a "failure." Nevertheless, acknowledging our share of responsibility in a failure of some kind can be a necessary (and usually painfully awkward) first step on the path to personal growth.

It took me ten years to take responsibility for my failed first marriage. Even though my husband at the time had a cycle of cheating and then asking forgiveness, I was the one who perpetuated the cycle too. I didn't nip it in the bud. I let it go on for years and years. In effect, that made me culpable too. When I finally owned up to it, I was much more able to get on with things. I had honored myself so little that I had allowed this behavior to control me far too long. There are always gifts given to us in both good and bad times. I brought forth two beautiful daughters into this life from that union, and for them I am forever grateful. It's a long process to learn to love yourself, but the love and unending patience of a good partner is the best support system I can think of. It's still something I work toward.

I think there are many around us who struggle to value themselves. That we have been courageous enough to come to this world again and again and work out the many kinks is not only brave and selfless, but what I believe we must do as growing spiritual beings. Knowing that I am loved and cherished each step of the way by so many beings has helped me to understand that I am not being judged for the flaws in my character, but loved and honored in spite of them.

Springtime here in the north woods of Idaho is full with nature's promise of rebirth. Our iced-over pond is once again a safe and warm haven for its many waking residents. The Cutthroats jump and splash about in an attempt to fill their long, empty bellies with all the sweet, tasty insects they can gulp. Our seven painted turtles (I tried to count them) gleefully stretch their dainty, snobbish necks toward the new warmth of the sun, and all around us is the soft, sweet smell of the earth.

We put on our tattered, fading overalls and big black rubber boots, drag out all the garden tools we've stored in the barn during the winter, and begin work on our large veggie garden and smaller flower gardens that we have dotted around the cabin. After a five-month hibernation in our tiny home, it's a welcome relief to work outside, even if it's in the muck of spring.

We spent the time wisely fertilizing, mulching, tilling, and weeding; but our sore bones and Mother Earth repaid us with a bountiful autumn harvest. The locals warned us of the occasional early frost that could wipe out some of the less hardy plants. Tomatoes, it seems, struggle to ripen in this environment, because the growing season is rather short, but so far, so good. We have learned which plants are the early, hardy ones. Our relationships are not unlike our gardens; they take time to prepare, constant care, and plenty of weeding and attention. I love Tom's garden analogies!

To create our most marvelous garden, there must be gardeners committed to the tedious task of weeding. It doesn't take long for a lush and lovely garden to become choked and infested by out-of-control weeds. A short time of neglect is all it takes before a simple task, like daily weeding, turns into a monumental chore.

It's a slow, insidious process as neglect replaces work. In a relationship, it's only a matter of time before indifference and laziness choke the life out of our love. Ego has no place in keeping life steady and calm. Oftentimes, one of us has to be the bigger of the two and look past the hurt and madness of things to try and smooth things away, or at the very least, try to start a conversation in that direction.

Usually one person takes on this task. I don't think that's exactly fair, but often it happens like that. For that person, semantics and patience are virtues that are most probably a good thing. Timing is everything. You know your mate, so don't make things worse. Replace that awful feeling that lurks in the pit of your gut when you are upset, with something that feels ever so much more loving and content. I can think of nothing better. I am not saying this is easy; it's not, but it's doable.

Misunderstandings cause so much heartache. I find it absolutely incredible that I can say something that is as plain as day to me, but Tom takes it a totally different way. It's mind-boggling! I know he'd say the same thing about me.

The world is nothing but a school,
Our relationships with our husband or wife,
With our children and parent

With our friends and relatives
Are the universities in which
We are meant to learn
What love and devotion truly are.

— S W A M I   M U K T A N A D A

Commitment is present in many aspects of our lives. We obligate ourselves to the workplace, charity, exercise, and any other number of worthwhile causes. Sadly, and all too frequently, the arenas of our lives that require us to be the most committed are often the most neglected.

This progressive, fast-paced world we've all shaped has made it nearly impossible not to neglect our lovers, children, friends, and family at some point. Regrettably, in the misguided effort to get more for the people we truly adore, we sometimes end up giving and receiving less.

I think commitment is a whole lot easier if I know there's an end to it. My whole premise is that the sooner I start a journey, the sooner it ends. This journey, however, is ongoing. There are plenty of times when I struggle with commitment.

Last month I promised myself I'd spend two hours each day on a needlepoint Christmas stocking for my grand-daughter, Tyler. I lasted four days. This is fairly typical behavior for me. I get bored, overdo it, and wear myself out, or get discouraged with my slow and unimpressive progress. In a beloved relationship, on the other hand there is no end to commitment, there are only beginnings.

It's an ongoing progression of adjustments as both partners grow and change. The point of such vigilance enables us to pay attention to each other and remain alert and focused on the important priorities of our union. To be watchful and caring to other's needs shouldn't be a burden. Above everything, there are the two of you.

I add my breath to your breath
that our days may be long
on this earth.

N A V A H O   P R A Y E R

Appreciation

A friend of mine once expressed how much he appreciated being appreciated. It struck a chord with me. How very easy it is to simply stuff appreciation under the table. Since then I've tried very hard to express my gratitude to everyone, but especially to Tom for all those easily overlooked things he does for me. Little things come to mind, like when he drains the honey jar and refills it, so that when I make myself a cup of tea I don't get all sticky and messy filling it up again.

I appreciate so much that he takes the time to turn on the light next to the bed so I don't kill myself going up to the loft after dark. These incidental and seemingly insignificant acts speak volumes to me. They tell me daily that I'm appreciated, and by expressing my thanks to him for his concern, I not only acknowledge his good deed, but also let him know how much I value and appreciate him too. The next time I'm happy to refill the honey jar.

I heard something on TV the other day that made me shake my head in disgust. A married couple, who were feeling the squeeze of their relationship, was befuddled as to why it wasn't working out well for them. What eventually came out was that neither valued the other's attempts at doing incidental things during the day. They were quite rude to each other. They didn't bother, it seemed, with the everyday courtesies. Being polite and considerate, saying "thank you" many times during the day, should be a given. It's just part of being kind. I'm thanked for each and every meal, good or horrid...wow!

Without kindness there is little to stand on, and being considerate is just obvious, isn't it? Little things make a big difference in relationships. At least they do for us.

There's no such thing as a perfect relationship, only those that look ideal from the outside in. There will always be the proverbial ebb and flow. That's the natural order of things, and that's fine. I don't really like a fight, but I won't shy away either. In years past, one couldn't say that about me, and I still get all queasy about confrontation, but if you can't face each other, discuss the immediate problem, and deal with it in a timely and adult manner, your day will be shot.

> *Love doesn't just sit there like a stone,*
> *It has to be made new,*
> *Like brick; remade all the time.*
> — URSULA K. LE GUIN

Most of us don't like or want confrontation either, but few if any are so fortunate to get what we want. We're different people, with wonderfully diverse opinions and outlooks that, in and of themselves, craft unavoidable clashes. Our blemishes are bound to erupt sooner or later. Even that incredibly beautiful, perfect couple down the street, who appears flawless and unflappable, may very well be secretly angry and miserable with each other. As a society, we're perversely obsessed with perfection, but still feel some masochistic need to create and maintain a glowing persona, even thought it's an obviously unattainable goal. I find this is true of many things….so silly!

Suppose you scrub your ethical skin

Until it shines,

But, inside there is no music

Then what?

K A B I R

Those Changing Looks

I'm as vain as the next woman, and watching my youth fade is not my idea of fun, but I don't have $7,000 or whatever it costs these days for a tuck here and there, so I just have to make the best of it. I'm so blessed that Tom looks past all the wrinkles and sags to the place that holds me close to his heart. There are some I look past too!

We're imperfect people, and as such our love needs to find a way to work around our apparent limitations. Sadly, we receive countless messages from our culture that generate profound pressure, within ourselves and within our relationships, to be everything to everyone and be beautiful about it! As if things weren't hard enough!

The media would also have us all believe we're a hideous bunch after thirty-five. One wrinkle, one extra pound, and we're immediately deemed expendable or unworthy. I noticed that most of the wrinkle cream commercials target 20 year olds....What's that about? Time to check the yellow pages for the nearest plastic surgeon! I must admit though that I tried some lip plumping cream just to see what would happen. My daughter, Christen and I had a good laugh over that one. Her lips blew up like a blow fish and mine did nothing. Money well spent!

The effort we put into staying the effects of time and conforming to a ridiculous standard of beauty seem, more often than not, to make us more paranoid, disgruntled, and unsatisfied with ourselves. This often leaves us empty and unable to appreciate the real and genuine beauty radiating within all of us. My goodness, we've gotten this all so upside down.

As our efforts to make over our exterior sabotage our inner beauty, these same dynamics work in a relationship...or against it. "Progress, not perfection;" so it follows that no couple can be perfect either. There's no miracle cream that can cure the lumpy, bumpy road to love. The miracle and the magic must come from both partners working hard and committing totally to making an amazing couple.

We have also known too many couples who have been together for countless years, but who really dislike and annoy each other. My ex-husband's grandparents were married for somewhere around sixty-five years. When Grandpa passed over some years ago, Grandma gave a sigh of relief and simply said, "I'm glad that's over with. I loved him, but he was a difficult, irritable man." Sixty-five years! Ugh!

It's hard to believe that much of the time, their generation endured marriage whatever the cost. For one reason or another they stayed together, and often ridiculed those who struggled in their marriages or had the courage to part ways and try once again for that elusive gift of love. It takes courage to let go. Commitment is obviously commendable, but not worth years of misery.

A scrumptious couple is a well-balanced one, each putting many gifts into the other's arms. But the best of couples usually go through absolutely awful days too. To survive them, they have to be prepared and equipped to see the hard times through to the good times. To overcome those inevitable troubles may take as little as a thoughtful note tossed in a lunch bag, or as much as setting aside that pride for a while and taking a good look within. There's so much at stake in a truly incredible couple.

Tom flaps around like a mad chicken when he's furious at me, and I tend to confront him, which makes him even crazier (I'm not always good at waiting for a better moment). It's probably a funny sight to see, though. If we weren't so embroiled in a good battle, we'd probably have a good laugh too. It's good to duel it out once in a while (I don't mean being physically or verbally abusive) provided it's not taken over the line and each can take something constructive from the argument and perhaps even resolve the problem.

So love is the treasure that we all can find. But love without commitment is analogous to a house of cards: when the winds of life blow, as they will most assuredly do, it will all come tumbling down around us if we aren't diligent in averting the very storms that would take us under.

There are many faces of commitment. It is a process; a lifelong process that at times will hold us softly, but at other times constrict and smother us. Nonetheless, if we choose to commit, we will have a partner with whom we can be closer to in this lifetime than anyone else. They are the ones we can laugh with, make love with, grieve with, and cherish until our dying time and beyond. There is nothing in the world more precious than the love of another human being. When all is said and done, the only thing left to us is what we carry within our hearts for one another.

May your love be firm,
and may your dream of life together
be a river between two shores—
by day bathed in sunlight, and by night
illuminated from within.
May the heron carry news of you
to the heavens,
and the salmon bring the sea's blue grace.
May your twin thoughts spiral upward like
leafy vines,
like fiddle strings in the wind,
and be as noble as the Douglas fir.
May you never find yourselves back to back
without love pulling you around
into each other's arms.

— J A M E S   B E R T O L I N O

Our first summer at Snowhawk was very pleasant. The days were often hot, up in the nineties, but the evening always brought cool relief. The forest here is dense and wild. The delicate foliage of the island is gone. In its stead are tall fir, hemlock, and cedars trees, all lining the horizon and dotted on occasion with soft deciduous cottonwood and beech trees. Tansies, lupines, and daisies blanket any open field. All around us we have mountains. There is no more oceanfront; in its stead we have a blessedly cool little pond, which is a welcome relief on those unbearably hot summer days.

Tom is in retirement heaven. His tractor is fast becoming an intrinsic part of life here. He spends hour after hour rototilling the gardens, and turning the root-bound, uneven soil into fine, well-draining earth.

As the days of summer progressed, they grew increasingly hotter. Thankfully, the air was dry enough so the humidity was inconsequential, and we always had our little pond for a brief swim or a long, leisurely float. This we often did in the buff, and although we had warned our neighbors and friends of this little ritual, oftentimes they would neglect to honk on the way down and get an eyeful…Oh well!

The pond quickly became the centerpiece of Snowhawk. Murphy would take huge leaps into the middle of it to retrieve a stick or ball, and Marley, who was older and could never seem to get to the ball or stick before Murphy, soon happily resigned himself to just swimming on his own, around and around in circles. One time a tiny green frog hoped on his back and enjoyed a lovely ride for quite a while. Silly boy!

On occasion, moose also seemed to enjoy the cool of the little pond, as well as, the taste and crispness of the lily pads I had so painstakingly buried in the muck at one end of it. I suppose it's a good thing they get the munchies once in a while, since lilies do tend to choke a pond after too long. It's, none the less, a bit unnerving to be swimming and have a moose join in!

Mama Moose and her baby came to the pond one morning. What a lovely and sacred sight. She watched so attentively as her baby learned to navigate the water and gently nudged her up the bank and out of the pond when they were done. As sweet as it was to have them there all summer, we had to be especially vigilant of the dogs because of the fierce protective nature of the mother moose. They have very poor sight, but a keen sense of smell, and they have a heck of a temper. We are the intruders here, so we are happy to share what we can. But sometimes it's a bit off-putting.

I planted a little willow in the front yard. Generally we have to keep a wire fence around a baby tree for quite a while so that it has a fair chance of growing without being eaten down to nubs. Once we removed the wire, all went well for most of the summer, until Mama Moose and her now older baby came for another swim and noticed my willow. Baby took one look at that tree and decided right then, it was snack time. Nothing deterred her. I boldly (some would say stupidly) yelled and waved my arms, and then got the hose out and sprayed her, but all I managed to do was piss her off. She jumped into the pond, which by now she was fully capable of swimming in, ran around its edge and right into my flower garden. I swear she looked up at me and defiantly jumped back over the fence and made for the willow again. I could do nothing. Slack jawed, I stared in disbelief. By now Tom was coming down the driveway, and honking the horn on the truck so that maybe mama moose would at least move (she was paying no attention to my tirade). This wasn't perhaps the smartest thing to do either, as a bad-tempered moose can turn on a car and easily cause lots of damage by stomping on it.

At any rate, they were undeterred, and so there was little to do but watch helplessly as my little tree was munched down to nothing! Such is life in Northern Idaho. Sometimes sharing is just not an option!

In mid-summer, the dragonflies start frequenting the pond. First to come for a visit are the Damselflies, the little delicate blue ones; I think they are the sweetest. Then come the Skimmers, the ones we call the biplanes because they are black and white and have the look of those planes. But toward the end of the summer come my favorite, the large turquoise-and-green winged kind called Blue-eyed

Darners that hover like helicopters and all buzz quickly from one end of the pond to the other, hoping not to get munched on by the ducks.

They enjoy inspecting us too, often staring at us full in the face. We must have passed inspection, because we seem to have a plethora of them about in the summer. They seem to especially like Tom, as they land on him endlessly. Between the hummers thinking his red cap is a big flower and the dragonflies grabbing a ride now and again, it is truly funny to see him walking around with these little creatures flitting about him. I'm only a little bit jealous!

Dragonflies are my very favorite type of insect. I don't know quite why, I have just always found them friendly and curious. They're ancient, magical creatures that fly between water and air. I think I'll get a tattoo of a dragonfly one day.

I left Snowhawk for a few weeks to help welcome Sawyer, our third grandchild, into this world and provide my daughter Christen some relief helping with the other two. It was very wonderful for me to be there. We now have a beautiful little new "chili bean" for a granddaughter. She was very red and had black hair when she was delivered; her mother looked the same except for the hair. Thus the nickname.

Tom had to stay home to tend the very parched gardens. One problem when you have so much outside work: it's hard to leave for any length of time unless you have someone willing to take time from their own day to learn Tom's elaborate system of hoses and Rainbirds. Dragging hoses every which way is tough and always, always maddening because they tend to kink up constantly. I really dislike hoses!

He loves hanging out at the cabin and much prefers not to leave the property, so he happily spent time weeding and water everything, every day. He took long walks in the woods and gathered all-important fire wood for the next winter. He was learning how to relax.

As the days grew hotter and hotter, the watering became more frequent. Eventually, our well tapped out and we were into sand. Once again we learned a bit more about our situation. It was clear that our big well, which had been driven down over two hundred feet, at a huge expense, was clearly not going to cut it. It brought up silt each time we taxed it a bit, so Tom had to hand dig another one for the garden water.

Keep in mind, we knew nothing about any of this. He chose an arbitrary spot behind the barn that he thought was convenient to the gardens, and it wasn't long before he, by shear chance, located an underground stream, set up a pump, stuck a sand point in the hole, and was back in the business of watering the plants. Not bad for city folk!

It isn't that people didn't tell us what to, or what not to expect, we just didn't ask the right questions...sort of like the bird seed and the bears. Much of living in the country is just finding things out by trial and error. The all-important word here is humor. You can find it everywhere...or not.

After I had been in town for the day, a wind storm came up. It was a fierce one too, some kind of mini-tornado, I heard. The trees on the road were bent at forty-five-degree angles, and I feared one would snap and come down on the car. I eventually got home safely, and noticed branches and large limbs strewn about. The grill had been blown off the porch, and the patio umbrella wasn't stuck in the picnic table any more. I set about to look for it, but since I couldn't see it anywhere, I was sure it had been blown into the woods....you never know. Finally I sat down on the deck to ponder this interesting dilemma when I noticed the smallest bit of the end of the umbrella pole sticking out from the middle of the pond! Ha! I had found it...so now, how to get it? I got into the canoe (I probably should have changed out of my good clothes) and paddled out to retrieve it.

Keep in mind, it was obviously upside down with the umbrella part opened! If the spirits and fairy folk were looking at this, no doubt they were having themselves a good laugh. I know I was. The canoe was tipping from side to side, and I was laughing my head off. The umbrella was not cooperating, full of water, and heavy. No one was around, just me in the middle of the pond, laughing hysterically and getting weaker by the minute from the laughing…

All ended well; the thing finally succumbed to my yanking on it and came out, none the worse for wear. I suppose I could have been furious, but what would have been the point? Some of my friends seem to think I have an odd sense of humor, but no matter. Looking at it, it was a funny sight!

This summer we bought three ducks, Dumbleduck, Rosie, and Gracie. Dumbleduck is a Cayuga, and the two girls are Blue Swedes. It's sweet to have them run about, but they do seem a bit messy. They seem messy a lot! Whereas last summer, the dogs had the run of the pond, this summer they will not. Dumbleduck is the boss. They've gotten so round and fat that they have a hard time waddling on land. No matter; Dumbleduck faithfully leads his little troupe down to the pond each morning, and somehow they find their way back to the coop at night. He's a bit of a tyrant. Unfortunately for Frodo, he got in Dumbleduck's way, and the nasty little duck grabbed hold of his ear and wouldn't let go. Poor Frodo just endured this misery until someone heard his whimpers and rescued him. The big dogs don't quite know where they stand with this little pack, although we think they suspect the worst. I think Rosie gets a bit frustrated with him too, and sets off on her own on occasion…as she should!

Tom spent the last month cutting and chopping wood. He has a fear of us freezing to death this winter. Since we are still new to this, we really don't have a clue how to judge how much wood we will need. With the endless stash of wood around here, he doesn't need to go very far to find fallen and dry trees.

In his haste and enthusiasm to prove himself a lumberman of some worth, he fell a tree on poor Gimili (the tractor), which thankfully only sustained a small crack. Tom managed to dive under it just in time. It's a story, not unlike the "fish story," that keeps getting better with age. They are both thankfully still working. I'm really lots happier just not knowing certain things.

I think the next time he tried to fell a tree, it landed on the one edifice in the near vicinity…the outhouse! Again, no casualties except for maybe an ego. Ha!

Deep listening is miraculous for both
listener and speaker.
When someone receives it with openhearted, non-judging, intensely interesting
listening, our
spirits expand.

S U E   P A T T O N   T H O E L E

Communication Glitches

It figures then that if commitment is the foundation of our house of love, communication is its framework. In keeping with the house analogy then, within the finished walls of any home there are beams, studs, insulation, and countless yards of wiring. All serve to create a structure that will house us in a comfortable, safe, and supportive way. In a relationship there are countless ways in which to communicate. Many are complicated, and often veiled, a bit like the framework around us. Each serves to either support or destroy the structure that houses our bodies and our souls.

Communication, or lack thereof, either serves to strengthen a relationship and connect the people involved, or tear it limb from limb. We seem to be best at all the direct and perhaps less subtle ways to communicate in the beginning of a relationship. It's still easy and light, uncomplicated and energized. Communication can be great in one area of our lives and miserable in another. Just because we seem to communicate where and how to pick up all three kids at the same time in different places is great, but sometimes it doesn't necessarily mean we can talk on a more casual or intimate level.

The really hard stuff is so often shoved aside and neglected. We need to embrace all levels of communication to create that incredible relationship we all hope for.

Our feelings are our reality. Whether or not our partners agree with them isn't the question. What we feel is real and true to us, and should be honored and addressed as such. Dismissing hurt feelings or what seems absolutely silly and inconsequential to us may have deep meaning to our mates. If allowed to go on unchecked, the repercussions will surely show up at some inappropriate time.

Some of us are delicate. We can't stand for someone to suggest a different means to an end. Some of us take things way too personally and refuse any honest and well-intentioned criticism. After a while it's just easier to ignore our sensitive partner and forgo a big flap about something rather than get into it and chance the consequences. Regrettably, all we end up doing, in that regard, is band-aiding a small problem, which invariably will fester later and cause even more grief—not unlike putting off cleaning the fridge for a few months…it can't be good!

There are even those walking among us who are so sensitive that even the slightest variation in their partner's mood or voice sends them reeling if they perceive even a hint of a problem stirring. I can't seem to have a nasty thought without apparently having it lit up like a neon sign over my head.

There are times when I'm livid about something or other, but choose to pick a better time to discuss it—a good practice on paper. Regrettably, since I seem incapable of hiding my feelings from most people, I don't get let off the hook easily. I can't really tell you if that's good or bad. Sometimes when I'm forced to blurt out my feelings without simmering for a bit, it causes more grief; other times it clears the air.

To be able and willing to communicate on a casual level is to be able to chat over dinner, joke around, laugh and play together, read to each other, and just be great if not best friends. Most of us can usually scope out the married couples in restaurants because they're usually the ones who sit like they're blobs, just eating and not saying much.

The business of running a household can create another communication nightmare of its own, especially if we're looking the other way. Money matters, paperwork, and the stress over whatever else gets mixed into it can really test our determination to work through our problems. Knowing what things to let go of is a skill that is acquired with experience. Fighting over every little thing goes nowhere at all.

Once again, it's compromise. I don't much like it either, and Tom's version of compromise can be for me to agree with him. But without it, we spin our wheels and get nowhere fast. So sometimes, as I said before, we often agree to disagree and allow each other to win from time to time.

Intimate communication can often be a most challenging undertaking too. If you can't effectively communicate on the other levels, it stands to reason that speaking deeply from your heart will be a bit of a stretch. Without a deep trust in each other and in your partnership, intimacy on every level is a nonissue. It's the element of communication where many of us feel most vulnerable.

To be truly in love, you must first be willing to open fully to the other. You must be willing to chance that the person you have chosen to be most personal with will allow for your imperfections, allow for your dreams to be heard, fears to be appreciated, and thoughts to be honored and respected. Without allowing for such trust, how can you be truly connected and be everything you should and can be?

The little games we play sometimes help to break the pattern of neglect. Tom loves badminton; he's obsessed with it, really. Sometimes this old body can beat him, and on those well-earned occasions I take full advantage of the prizes! It's a full ten minutes of doing, with me, whatever I want to do: no arguments, no fussing or fuming, just lovely time alone together.

It would be lovely if he was more willing to do my bidding on a more regular schedule, but he isn't, so this is the answer—games! We generally play games, and whoever wins gets ten minutes of whatever he or she wants. There is a time limit to this, though; usually this is only good for the day, and usually you can only piggyback two or three wins at a time. You have to have some rules.

Communication is a work in progress, and the peaks and valleys that we all seem to go through from time to time should be recognized as places of potential growth. Without the cooperation of both people, there will be no communication strong enough to carry us through the maze of emotions we all seem destined to wade through.

The early stages of a relationship are charged with an intensity born in the newness and novelty of a budding love. After all, at this point in time, what is there really to lose?

After time that heightened sense of newness, plus the ability we had to overlook small irregularities in each other, is less effective, allowing the light to dawn and the true nature of the beast to stand up and be counted. Resentment and indifference can start to rear their miserable heads.

As relationships continue, many settle into comfortable routines. Life carries us along, and we busy ourselves with the day's many wonders. Unfortunately, communication in many of its forms can, all too often, slow down or disappear altogether. It requires constant vigilance to notice the warning signs of comatose communication and to try very hard to wake it up the best way we know how.

Familiarity can breed contempt, but more often it provides a fertile ground for apathy. The apathy found in many relationships is a very subtle force, working quietly and usually undetected as it alters and shapes our connections.

Lovers have, and should use, an abundance of ways to communicate: touch, body language, dress, eye contact, gestures, and the traditional written and spoken world. Most of us can already appreciate that the most powerful communication tool of all is body language. A look doesn't often lie or exaggerate the truth; it cuts to the quick and can say a thousand worlds in an instant. A good scowl—thankfully, not usually from my husband—has sent me fleeing the room many a time (ugh, the many memories of childhood). So often what and how we feel is what's left to us after all those words have vanished from our minds.

There are so many times when this commanding force is working to sustain or destroy our commitment. All of the feelings we gather from our mates are likely the direct result of a barrage of small daily messages we exchange between each other. The occasional grandiose gestures of a big bouquet of roses or a diamond bracelet only work to enhance a relationship already in bloom and fully backed up by those wonderful small messages given daily that cost nothing. The impact of such flamboyant gifts fade if, after the petals have wilted, so too has the attentiveness of our mates.

Taking the time to appreciate our mates in any small way will make us the heroes. The simple act of helping with a chore, or acknowledging the other's efforts, a small sweet gift, or Tom saying those few dreamy words, "I love you, and you are important to me," say volumes to me.

There are some things we just have to let go of. Expending energy on issues that are really, in the long run, superficial, is just counterproductive. As an example, after Tom retired from the Navy, he was able to finally stop shaving. He also grew his hair and pierced his ear. He transformed himself from a clean-cut naval officer to someone the kids called the "Happy Hippy." People have been seen crossing the street to avoid him! He looked like he needed a number on the back of his shirt. But even though I prefer the clean-shaven look, I've come to accept what he likes and needs. I tried complaining, but it really did no good, so I have asked that he at least keep all that hair clean and brushed. He tries.

I told him I love him for his beautiful soul and not his hair (I had to tell myself that one too). I love that he is happy and content within himself, doing what he chooses with his life, regardless of how he looks to others. We communicate many things and create the feelings that define our relationship as we move though our days together.

Our choices are much different from those of most people we know, but the issues we bring up are as valid for two old fools in the woods as they are for people juggling big careers, children, and the pressures of making ends meet.

It amazes me that Tom adores seeing me covered in dirt, hat askew, sitting in the garden digging potatoes. I hate digging potatoes. It's hard, boring work, so I'm usually in a foul mood, but I try to direct my misery at the spuds and not at Tom. This is always easier to do when he appears with a cool drink and we sit quietly in the warmth of the garden for a few minutes of rest. I love this man!

The same is true when I see him working hard at cutting and chopping endless cords of wood for the chilly winter nights that seem so far away in the heat of the summer sun. The work is backbreaking, and at times it seems the last potato and the final cord of wood will never be gathered and finished. All is made easier and more pleasant when we take the time to acknowledge each other's efforts, if only with a dirty smile and cold drink.

It takes plenty of effort to remember the little things that make life pleasant. Sometimes I get upset and say something merciless when I should have bitten my tongue. Sometimes I just have to shake my head and keep quiet, as does he. We are not in a battle, and no one person has to win. Yes, for the sake of quiet sanity, I think we both allow the other his or her way on occasion. We handle arguments differently. I tend to be the one who wants to hash it out; Tom usually wants to run…literally!

Eventually, we either compromise or Tom huffs out to the barn and sits in the cold until he can't stand it any longer, or he hangs out on the deck smoldering and muttering to himself until he calms down (keep in mind there is no place to hide in a five hundred square foot house). I refuse to go to the barn. There is just no getting around those differences of opinion. We just have to work them through, agree to disagree, and get on with it.

A walk in the woods, a drive to the little general store a few miles away for an ice cream, or a float in the pond are all ways to recognize and share our delight with life's little joys and the pleasure we find in each other. There is absolutely no sense in staying angry. It is a waste of energy and dulls those beautiful days.

Life is a precious and fragile thing that can too easily be snatched away from us in a moment. We work hard to remember that and count all our blessings. Learning not to irritate the heck out of each other doesn't hurt either. Over the years we've learned how to pick and choose our battles. Discussions about ex-spouses and the death penalty are usually taboo in our family.

Sometimes, rather than be cranky with Tom, I ensconce myself in the kitchen. Unfortunately, cooking for two, one of whom is on a perpetual diet, can undermine the whole purpose of dieting. I love to cook (well, that may be an exaggeration). It used to be that after a long day at work, I'd get home and aimlessly prepare a quick meal. Now I spend prolonged periods of time in front of the stove, baking fresh breads and cookies and trying out any number of interesting new recipes. Thus the problem—even a mediocre chef must ensure quality control. The manifestation of my problem is eleven pounds in three months! Sadly, there doesn't appear to be a light at the end of the tunnel.

Tom has even suggested cookware with locks. Very funny! It's now my challenge to overcome this new and distressing habit.

Yesterday I made something I call raspberry cream. It's one of those recipes that can't be easily cut in half. We were therefore left with eight cups of the stuff, each with its share of fattening calories. They naturally got stuffed in the fridge, just waiting for me to get even remotely near them. Tom only nibbles on sweets, so most things I make are left for me to do with as I may. Of course, even though many things I enjoy doing during the day don't require me to be near the fridge, I still find myself drawn like a magnet to it.

The fridge lures me to it as if it were playing sweet flute music. I know I need balance in my life—we all do— but oh well; I'll get it later. This new adventure we are on now demands it. I am doomed! In these little silly ways I'm being taught how to live within the boundaries of my own self and to take the freedom I now enjoy and learn how to play within its very real limitations.

For those less challenged in this area or who have a large family to take up the slack: enjoy, enjoy! Most of the time we eat fresh, organic, healthy food, but into each life a little decadence must creep.

Raspberry Cream

This is a recipe developed over time by a number of my girlfriends. We first tasted something like this in a wonderful little restaurant on Whidbey Island in Washington State. Because the proprietors were, understandably, reluctant to divulge the ingredients, we all went to work and drew from countless resources to come up with this recipe. This rich confectionary takes very little time to prepare and is most beautiful when served in crystal stemmed dessert dishes. Its white cream with red raspberries on top is a truly lovely holiday delight.

Ingredients
2 cups heavy whipping cream
1 pkg. gelatin in ¼ cup warm water
¾ cup sugar
1 tsp. vanilla
1 cup plain yogurt
1 cup sour cream
sweetened frozen raspberries

In a medium saucepan over low heat, mix one envelope of gelatin in the warm water until dissolved. This is tricky so stir it in very slowly and carefully so there are no clumps. If by some chance you do get some clumps you will have to use a strainer and put your pudding through it…Stir in the heavy cream and mix well. When this is done and the cream is still only warm (don't get it too hot), pour the sugar in and stir until dissolved. Take off the heat and pour in the vanilla, yogurt, and sour cream. Stir well with the whisk until everything is very smooth and a bit thick. Chill overnight and top each serving with two tablespoons of raspberries (in the freezer section of your grocery story) right before serving. Yield: 4 cups. I serve only about ½ cup per person because it's so rich.

Life is not a race.
But a journey to be savored
Each step of the way.
Yesterday is history
Tomorrow is a mystery
And today is a gift.

— UNKNOWN AUTHOR

Some mornings one of us wakes up cranky, but regardless of our moods, someone has to put aside the grumpiness long enough to at least acknowledge, in a pleasant way, the other's existence. It sets the mood for the entire day! Once again we make a choice. It's up to us to create harmony or misery. If something is getting your goat from the previous day, then arrange a time during the day to talk it over. Don't let things bog down; they'll come out sooner or later, and usually later will be worse.

Bad news doesn't get better with age.

— OLD CHINESE PROVERB

Putting someone immediately on the defensive won't work either. How you choose to approach your conversation is going to keep the doors open or shut them down. We are both becoming more aware of the benefits of semantics and listening to how we talk to the other.

I can't tell you how many times Tom will say, "You sounded grumpy or irritated with me," when, in fact, I wasn't at all. I enjoy a good discussion, but sometimes he thinks of my discussions as arguments. He's not one to allow me a bad mood either. He prefers that I am happy 100 percent of the time, which of course is not remotely realistic. I have learned to make my intentions crystal clear, but it has been hard for me. He is learning to accept that I can have bad moods and still love him…imagine that!

Somewhere along the line, he equated someone who is unhappy with him to someone who doesn't love him. Although that may have been the case in times past, I have to be aware of this particular glitch in his thinking and reassure him, over and over, that I do, in fact, love him, although I may not be happy with a certain behavior of his at the moment. This is something I will most likely continue to do, as these wounds from his past go very deep and they are not diminished quickly.

Honestly, men are a different breed. My friends and kids seem to be able to catch each other's thoughts before they're said. We seem to instinctively know what we each mean. For example, if I point to a particular tree and say something like, "Do you see that bird?" They'll seem to know exactly what tree I am pointing at. This is not true about Tom and me. I've learned to be specific, so I say something like, "Wow! Look at that tall cedar, the one with the dead part in the middle and standing next to the sign near the pond." Phew! It makes me nuts, but it's a small price to pay for peace. Little things!

Agree to disagree—just don't create a Grand Canyon of emotional issues by tossing your feelings into an abyss where they are never dealt with in any way. Then, before you realize it, you'll be standing on opposite sides of the canyon, unable to see or hear each other. Prior to choosing this particular tactical move, look hard at yourself and see if you are doing all you can to promote healthy discussions. Listen to your words and the emotions you put behind them. Watch what your body is saying, hear the tone and inflections in your voice, and ask yourself if you're sending the message you had intended.

Often our garbled attempts at communication are misinterpreted because of our lousy delivery and indifference. You can bet that many times, what we have intended to say gets interpreted in a whole different way, and it's usually not a favorable one. So take responsibility for communication or the lack thereof.

How well we communicate has, perhaps, the most powerful daily effect on how we give and receive love. A loving greeting and departure are less subtle, but nonetheless speak volumes.

How does it feel to leave the house in silence and return home to even more silence—or worse, a running account of the day's tragedies without so much as a nod? Does it make you want to rush home the next day? We're not campaigning for you to greet your sweet mate with a surprise party (unless it's his birthday) or a spectacular display of over–the-top affection, but a few warm moments and a hug isn't going to kill either of you and may even make for a really pleasant evening. Share that wonderful small, safe haven in each other's arms that you found years before.

Feeling safe enough as a couple to talk over all that needs to be said is the cornerstone of communication. We're lost without it. On occasion, buried feelings may be best left alone, as we have already said, but more often than not, they need to be exhumed and faced head-on. The baggage we carry with us can be enormous, overwhelming, and can often have an unhealthy way of blocking the very essence of a good union. I have never been able to outrun my issues, nor have I been able to bury them. It's some kind of cosmic law that to grow and become stronger people, we have to turn around and face the enemy.

Let's be realistic. If the boundaries you've jointly established have been in some way compromised by one person, then all bets are off. Every couple conducts its relationship the way it feels most comfortable. Use whatever information you can gather from different sources that you think can help, and let go of the rest. Not everything works for everyone. If you're happy, then you're obviously doing something right. Congratulations! If you're miserable and want your relationship to work better, then make a deliberate decision to be happier and do the work it will require together. Remember, it takes both of you for this. If a marriage counselor will help, why not try one?

It's a fact that at times we're not all delightful people. On those rare occasions that you feel especially mean-spirited or irritable for no particular reason, direct your wrath at an inanimate object and not at your poor, unsuspecting mate or the pet. Take a walk alone and find a solitary place of your own, be with yourself, and give yourself the gift of compassion. If you have to scream, then try doing it into a pillow, or cup your hand over your mouth and have at it. Vibrations are healing to a degree; just don't overdo it. A really good sound therapist can work wonders too; it usually makes me feel temporarily better! Allow yourself to feel why you're in such a bad mood. If you need time to grieve, take it. Acknowledge and honor your feelings: they are real and they are yours. When the time is right for you, do the work around them. If that means finding a good psychotherapist or just time to think things through, do it. And then continue on your amazing life.

If it's been a while and you're both feeling as if the other is a stranger, albeit a very nice one, try this little survey to reintroduce yourselves.

Change is a fact of life, no matter how we may resist it, no matter how much we both consciously and unconsciously try to ignore it. Change is always, always present in our lives. It may roar into our lives quickly and full in our faces, like death, or a career change, or it may be more subtle. It's the latter we fail to notice until we start feeling their pain.

Life happens along, and we start listening to different music and wearing different types of clothes. Our taste in food changes, and the perfume we once thought so fragrant now makes us nauseous.

This simple little exercise can be as powerful as it is easy to do. Just fill in the blanks, answer the questions, and spend some time together going over what you have discovered about the other that you had forgotten or just didn't know. Keep it nearby; it may come in handy someday.

It doesn't have to cost a small fortune to treat your mate beautifully. Be creative, have fun, and reconnect! Make up your own list of things too.

Our Romantic Survey

Favorite meals _____

Favorite color _____

Favorite drinks _____

Favorite restaurant _____

Favorite snacks/candies _____

Favorite places to go _____

Favorite vacation spots _____

Favorite perfume _____

Favorite thing to do with you on a rainy day _____

Favorite movie _____

Favorite flowers _____

Favorite holiday _____

Favorite book _____

Favorite author _____

Favorite games _____

Favorite store _____

Keep going!

The second part of this little survey may take a bit more time. Answer the questions with as much detail as you wish. You may sit and write them out alone, or take time to find a cozy place to sit and discuss them together. Don't answer the questions if you don't care to, and don't forget to add your own.

1. Describe a cherished moment in your life.

2. What is your ideal date?

3. What is your favorite thing to do on a date?

4. What does romance mean to you?

5. Name a place where you've always wanted to go.

6. Define intimacy.

7. Define who you think you are.

8. What are the priorities in your life?

9. Do you think you are doing enough together, and if not, how can you make more time for just the two of you?

10. Do you think you communicate well? If not, what can you do to improve it?

11. Do you think you have enough fun together? If not, how can you change that?

Over time, that favorite color may have changed, or the favorite dinner may now be too fattening. Use this survey to reacquaint yourself with the little things about each other that perhaps you've forgotten, or that have changed since you last asked. Be creative with the results. Have his favorite music softly playing when he gets home, or remember her with a special flower she loves. I always love the little sticky notes placed on my computer! Take the time to care. Taking the time, in and of itself, says a whole lot, so don't forget the thank-yous. Remember too, it's all about the little things.

I'm not talking sex here, although there's that too. I'm strictly sticking to the little sweet bits of warmth and tenderness that we women just can't seem to do without…nor should we. Oh, they are so sweet! Tom always remembers me with a little something that I just love. It doesn't have to be diamonds, but it has to be something he knows I would really like. He does it all the time. I am so lucky!

There are plenty of things we can do that are affectionate. Obviously, the usual things are the most desirable, but I think the all-important ones are the little ones that can make us feel so needed, loved, and appreciated.

It's so easy to let these sorts of things just drift away. They are so easy to go, but so very hard to get back. It's just another one of those essential things on that crowded to-do list.

Affectionate gestures of flowers and a dinner out are lovely—I would never say they aren't—but to me, and for me, the ones I need the most are the ones that require some sort of body contact. It may well be that our great passion has slipped a bit, but surely there is something to be gained by both from a gentle hug, a soft kiss, and the ever-romantic gesture of hand-holding. For women, and the occasional man, this is going to add up to sheer bliss!

Saying, "I love you" each day, making some sort of contact each day, and making the effort each day to attend in some way to your spouse will only rebound on you in many other wonderful ways.

Often who and what we have in our lives goes unnoticed and is pushed aside after a while. It's just a fact of life: we get busy and tend to under-appreciate and ignore that which we most cherish because we just take for granted too many things. The most effective way that we can think of to combat the insidious infection of indifference, which begins to erode any relationship over time, is effective communication. It seems that, all too often, many of us start taking our vital, precious gifts for granted.

The process of building our home taught us, in a simple and direct way, how not to take even the most ordinary things for granted: things like electricity, running water, refrigeration, and flush toilets. We are really all so spoiled. After three months of living in a dirty, musty barn, using the outhouse and rigged-up sink in the backyard, not to mention the not-so-toasty baths in the pond, we found ourselves staring with utter joy and awe at the sights and sounds of a functioning bathroom. We delighted over a brand-new kitchen sink with running water too!

Looking around, we have so much to be thankful for!

When you commit to a Spiritual partnership
You learn the value of considering the other position.
By becoming the other person, by truly walking into the fears of the
Other and
Then returning into your own being again.
You see each other through
The areas that require healing in each of you.

GARY ZUKAV

Gratitude and Acceptance

Y ears after building our house, we still remain grateful that we now have the simple fundamentals that make life so much more pleasant. We also appreciate that so many don't enjoy such things.

Having gratitude for all we have, plus trying hard to accept each other as we are, is something we strive really hard to achieve. There is, more often than not, that little nagging irritation inside that just wants to change this or that little thing about our spouse. If only he could be like this or she could be like that...Obviously, in a healthy relationship there has to be a good deal of acceptance. Acceptance for who we really and truly are. It is for sure a most important and necessary ingredient.

Trying to change someone is mostly impossible. But we all have a profound effect on those we live with. I know people who bring out my worst character flaws and those who make me a kinder and better person for just knowing them. I change my behavior by simply knowing them. Accepting our mates for who they are allows for the possibility that unconditional love, or something close to it, can really flourish. And who knows? Maybe those changes we want so much will just happen on their own. One can hope.

We know this can be a somewhat imperfect theory, although it sounds good. On one side, it seems like we should be totally accepting of our partners in all respects, including their special personal quirks. Embrace the goodness and joy we find in them, as well as the really gross or irritating stuff—I think not! Blind acceptance of these irritations, no matter how small, can quickly lead to yet another pile of pent-up frustrations and resentments. These, in turn, start the erosion process going full-bore. If we both make an attempt to respect the wishes of the other, especially the more obvious ones, it seems the road trampled would be far less bumpy.

All of us reach a point in our dealings with others when putting up with the quirky habits and small annoyances is done at a personal cost. If kept bottled up inside us, often our mounting unhappy feelings can explode with the simple ignition of a small, unrelated incident. We call it the blinker syndrome.

A close friend of mine was irritated by the fact that his wife didn't use her car's blinker while turning a corner. It turns out he was not angry about the blinker as much as he was ready for a good fight about something else she had done. If you feel an unreasonable anger over a simple oversight or small unintentional mistake on the part of your mate, perhaps there is something else at the core of your anger. Chances are it has absolutely nothing to do with forgetting to put the blinker on.

Holidays

S o for Christmas Eve, Tom is watching a football game with Mike, our neighbor, whose TV broke this morning and who frantically called to beg our couch for the game. I have a way-too-big turkey in the oven, and I'm about to go start the rolls. I've prepared too much food again for just the four of us. I don't have the hang of this yet. Thankfully our son, Sam, has come for a few days. He seems to have an inexhaustible appetite, so at least I won't have to cook again for days!

The Snowhawk sign at the entrance to the driveway has been bedecked with a mantle of cedar branches tied with a big red bow. Tom's twinkle lights just seem to make the cabin look magical and inviting, and I've made two wreaths for the doors from cedar, fir, and pine branches.

Christmas morning was no different than most. We got up and started a fire to warm the always-chilly cabin. Tom is just not a Christmas kind of guy. I think it's a sad reminder of his past, and I try to honor his feelings. He makes an effort, though, to honor mine, and tries in his own unique way to find little nice gifts.

We keep to a fairly strict budget when it comes to most things, and Christmas gets included in that too. It's just a part of life now. We accept it fully. Neither of us needs much of anything, so little sweet things work well for both us. Mostly now we buy for the kids and grandkids.

I really appreciate it when he finds a little something he remembered that I wanted. He keeps an eye out all the time for little things he knows I like. These are the things I really appreciate about him. Always, always, throughout the year he brings me home goodies from the store at the end of our road. He may be challenged in the holiday gift arena and may need to work just a tad harder at it, but he sure makes up for it with his other thoughtful gestures.

Before we open our little stash, we let the dogs have their stockings. Between all the dogs and George, there are toys strewn all over the place. Frodo is usually in doggie heaven, happily disemboweling each and every stuffed toy. Marley and Murphy have each already gobbled up their treats, and George is hiding somewhere from all the fuss. All is well with the world!

Seems strange, but I want a pretend tree this year. Here we are surrounded by a forest, and I want to march downtown to Ben Franklin and buy a plastic tree. I just think it's hypocritical to chop down another sweet little tree for two weeks of essentially celebrating life and all it bestows on us. I found a funny one with a too-big trunk and irregular branches sticking out from it. I don't think it's intended to look remotely like a real tree, but I think it works just fine.

Anyway, I still have a box of tinsel that I've saved from last year. My father loved tinsel. He thought a tree was not complete without the stuff, so I put a little on each year for him.

Christmas was always wonderful at my house when I was a child. We got to open our gifts on Christmas Eve because, in my mother's family, that's what they did. It was the one day when I really enjoyed my family. The one day I seemed to relax and enjoy the parties and the people. Dad went to elaborate measures to ensure that I believed in Santa too.

We had large doors that separated the living room from the dining room. The tree was in the living room and the presents (from mostly friends) were always neatly placed under it. I was never allowed to see my parents put anything under the tree unless it was something from a relative or friend. Of course, I was one of those kids who opened all my gifts beforehand and then neatly wrapped them back up so that I could look shocked and surprised on Christmas Eve when we opened them. Sadly, I have not changed my ways.

But the best part was trying to catch Santa in the act. I knew our house was his first stop, since miraculously everything turned up before Christmas morning, but how to catch Santa in the act?

Dad figured I would try desperately to stay awake until midnight. Usually I didn't make it. I know he spent lots of time happily scheming how to cheat me out of the discovery of the century!

One year I remember looking under the door. There were big black boots shuffling about near the tree! Could it be? He was always one step ahead of me! I don't remember when I finally found out about Santa, but it was quite a bit later than I care to admit.

My son, Sam, on the other hand, had that inkling about Santa when he was around seven. Seems Santa's handwriting looked a lot like mine...that was a flaw! We even had a friend dress up like Santa and visit us! Still, we could see the wheels turning in that little suspicious head of his.

Now, this kid was some sort of a little electronic genius at the ripe old age of two. By seven he was convinced he could wire the whole house and save us money.

Who needed an electrical contractor when we had him? (We were building our house on the island at the time.) So, now Santa was going to be in his crosshairs! He got out the video camera, stuffed it inside a planter on the piano, which happened to be exactly across from the staircase, and let it roll for hours.

The next morning, bright and early, he came bounding into our room, happy as could be with himself, and announced that he had indeed caught Santa in the act. Yup, there he was, after a couple of hours of blank tape, coming down the stairs with gifts in hand, so much for childhood fantasies. He was pretty proud of himself, but I think he was also one very disappointed kid.

Holidays can be so happy, but oftentimes they can be terribly sad too. In our family, the girls went here and there when they were young. I hated to see them have to shuffle between homes. On those years when they were "there," my heart broke in a million pieces. Our family was just not complete during those times, but it was the way it had to be. What we personally want doesn't always happen. There are just those times when our feelings just don't come first. Divorce takes such a toll on everyone.

Now, all in all, holidays are fine. The kids all seemed happy to be where they are and called with well wishes. I miss them all terribly, but I know they are happy and on their own adventures and I get to have my best friend with me. I feel incredibly blessed that we are all healthy and happy and after all, I think those are the top priorities.

Tom got his hand caught in the icemaker this morning—pretty funny, really (he wasn't hurt). I was more concerned with my melting coffee ice cream than with his poor squashed fingers. They came out eventually though, and I didn't have to call 911. I always wondered if they would be able to even find our cabin anyway.

The Christmas Wren

Snow was falling now. There was so much of it, in fact, that the snow lining the paths was taller than I was. The paths were becoming increasingly narrower, a phenomenon that apparently happens when gobs of snow can't be easily moved.

I felt so sorry for all the little critters of the forest though. I could do little for most of them now, but I thought I could at least keep filling the bird feeders and place peanuts under the old fir tree behind the house for the squirrels. Bear was sleeping now so there was no worry that they would be near the house.

The birds flocked to fill their bellies, and the little squirrel that lived in the crooked tree near the marsh ran up on occasion to steal a lovely peanut and carry it home to her nest. She was still mindful of George lurking about. Luckily for the birds, he was well content to stay in the warmth of his bed most days.

The feeders swung on a pole that Tom had stuck in the ground just outside the kitchen window so I could watch the birds feed while preparing the meals. We have bird houses stuck on most of the fence posts, and here and there on the cabin too. With so much snow now accumulating on their little roofs, they all looked as if they had lopsided top hats on.

One particular snowy day, I was making Tom his favorite chocolate-chip raisin cookies, and noticed a chubby Winter Wren sitting under the feeder. Tom laughed and said she was so fat that she could hardly move, and that was why she never jumped up on the feeder to eat. She waited and waited for bits of seed to drop into the snow beneath it.

Day after day the little wren sat, very contentedly, under the feeder. Thankfully, the cat never really noticed her. At first I thought that she might be stuck, or hurt because she never seemed to leave the little snow nest she had made for herself, but then I remembered that perhaps she preferred to scavenge on the ground for seed. Fat or skinny, maybe that was her preference.

When I woke up Christmas morning, I went to look out the window again and, sure enough, she was in her little nest, buried to her chest and looking quite content and ready for the new day. She hung out there for a good long time. She was a sweet sight that greeted me each morning.

Winter continued on her way. There were bright, sunny days and days full of snowy skies. Tom made sure the little cabin stayed warm and cozy. There were good books to read, puzzles to do, and quiet times to be had. When the snows finally stopped and the buds started to pop out in the springtime, our little Christmas wren, now off in the woods, would still, on occasion, came to sit under the feeder. No other wren ever came to visit that winter.

I for one wish we were not so remote and the roads were not so impassable. Driving is difficult at best, and for those who don't live here, it can be pretty gruesome. It's much more reasonable for the kids to visit in the summer when they can move about more easily, but I still like the notion of everyone together for the holidays, still I know it's impractical given where we are now. The weather is dreadful, the flights are expensive and everyone is stressed and uncomfortable. Our one blessing is that our son, who lives only a train ride away, manages to break away from his busy life on most holidays and spend some time decompressing here with us. An amazing gift!

But both of us, I think, are sad that the time with our young kids is over. I for one wish I could be surrounded by my family more than we are. It is a struggle for me sometimes. Tom is very much more able to handle all this, but misses his kids too. I am fortunate that he is, nevertheless, aware of my feelings and really makes a lovely effort to make the season bright.

I suppose some people whose kids are gone and who find themselves sort of at odds with the season may tend to let some of the more delightful, traditional parts of their holidays slip away too. I still do many of the same old things. I like the house smelling like cinnamon; I like Christmas music and candles around the house too. I love a good (fake) tree, cookies, fudge, and a big turkey.

Even if this is just for ourselves and friends, and may even feel a bit extravagant, it's still something I think is important to continue. Chapters open and close so often in all of our lives that this bit of nostalgia, for us, keeps us connected, in a small way, to all that was and still is.

Whatever your belief system, it is still a time for counting the many blessings we still have in our lives.

Creativity flourishes in an atmosphere
of safety and acceptance.
JULIA CAMERON

Imagination & Creativity

Imagination and creativity should be a wonderfully fun part of any relationship, and probably something we try to embrace since we're all alone here…and going only the slightest bit insane. I think I only speak for myself here.

Tom and I have both been blessed with a goodly amount of energy. Tom is a bit more fearless than I, and he is therefore happy to trudge through the woods regardless of the occasional bear, cougar, or moose. He is usually well-prepared with bear spray and his .45. I am not so happy to do this in the spring and summer, but he usually convinces me to go with him anyway. In the winter months it's nice to get the snowshoes on and take those walks; we get a good workout and rarely see any large animals, and I am always taken aback by the incredible beauty of the forest.

Last May Tom picked up an old guitar at a pawnshop in town and is taking a stab at playing. Let's not limit ourselves because we think we're adults and adults shouldn't do new and fun things.

Age is just a number. I feel like a young woman inside. I have to remind myself sometimes that I'm considered an elder. I think with age comes the blessed ability to care less and less about what others think. I climb trees, I play in piles of leaves, and I love ice cream cones! We won't even go into how I dress! Needless to say, my girls are generally horrified by my lack of taste in clothes, but most of the time have the good graces not say anything much. So what if I have a rather weathered old body on the outside? Inside I'm only twenty! That's just how it is.

Some of us tend to be a bit more conservative in our approach to fun. Gift yourself the permission to be silly and frivolous some of the time…and laugh, laugh, laugh. It does wonders for your physical health, as well as, your state of mind.

Just last week we went skating on our little pond. It was really quite enjoyable and my very creative husband even videoed us thrashing about on the ice. He even managed to hook up some sort of background music to the video. We only fell a couple of times and laughed continually. We tried to send the video to our kids but couldn't figure out how to compress it, so we ended up posting it on YouTube so they could see it. Somehow it got posted with the wrestling videos..sigh! Technology just isn't our thing.

We're all capable of creative self-expression. Don't relegate creativity only to the domain of artists, musicians, and writers. Each one of us has a creative side. Some of us just have to dig a bit deeper to come up with those impressive creations. Keep in mind, every bit as important as the inspiration itself is the desire and commitment to follow through. Being spontaneously creative is delightful, but planning a lovely event can be just as nice.

Last summer Tom took me to a secret knoll near the river's edge for a romantic little picnic lunch. At the time, he was being spontaneous, but he could afford to be, because a month or so earlier he had thought to gather the little necessities for such an exquisite, impromptu expedition. He didn't have to fumble around in the barn for a picnic basket since he already scoped out one earlier.

Our blanket was in it, and so were the paper plates and wine glasses. About the only thing he really had to think about when he picked out a time for all of this was the food. Think ahead and you'll be safe and very much appreciated for your efforts. I couldn't have been happier.

To dance naked under the stars is to shine as the
brilliant creations that we are.

— UNKNOWN AUTHOR

There are all sorts of fun thing to do in life, and most only contribute to a better and more fulfilled relationship. After several years of partnership and the joys of child rearing, romance can fade into oblivion. It's the fault of exhaustion and overextension. But romantic rigor mortis, unlike the real thing, can be revived.

It often takes a blend of imagination and commitment to bring life back to the romantic dead among us. Being creative can stimulate our otherwise bored and neglected love lives.

The ability to stretch and change may just generate a direct, new current of life into our otherwise lackluster unions.

Striving to enact a change in our partnerships isn't only up to our mates; it's up to us too. How each of us conducts his or her life bears fully on those around us. In turn, we may well see some noticeable improvements in how our partners and others interact with us.

Altering old habits is tricky, so there's no need to put yourself in a position to fall short of your mark. If you're not used to doing the little things and being romantic, then start slowly…at least it's a beginning. I guarantee, unless all is lost, those little gestures of good will can start the ball rolling again. It can't hurt.

Be with your partner, enjoy the time you have been given, and express your feelings. The gift of time is more precious than gold, and these days, that's saying something!

The holiday season has crept up on us with relentless, catlike sneakiness. We're going to have to find our own ways to celebrate without kids again. It is a time to challenge our own creativity and fill the void left by years of old traditions suddenly gone. It's important to make this special time joyful, instead of empty and sad.

Try something new
Dare to be foolish

As is in keeping with our own beliefs, we celebrate simply and enjoy the rich bounties of our forest rather than of the local department store. When the kids were young we both did things lots differently, but now we have a new way of expressing this season.

We bedecked our little tree with a sweet garland of dried cranberries and popcorn, bundles of tiny twigs tied with red raffia, and a few cherished ornaments.

To keep the dryness from the air, I always keep a tiny teapot boiling on the stove, stuffing cloves and cinnamon and some bay leaves into it daily. It fills the air with a steady stream of luscious scents and gives some moisture back to the dry winter air.

We have garlands of cedar across our front door, but I did get fake greens for the mantel, as I've learned from experience that the real stuff dries out too quickly. I'm also afraid I'll neglect a candle and it will burn down the house.

Tom put up icicle lights around the cabin again and strung some lovely colored lights in a little tree we planted next to the driveway. At night the motion light from the barn shines on the pond, which has turned into a delightful little skating rink. I imagine that to some this may seem as if we do very little, but to us, it is exactly what the season offers. It's our own way of creating a cozy space for us and our kids when they do come visit. Create the seasons in your life with love and imagination. Keep what you both hold so dear and don't let it slide away.

You have to work a little here. What may work for one couple could be absolute misery for another. We happen to enjoy a variety of activities, and usually aren't bashful about trying something new—you know, like playing darts for treats (wink, wink!).

Some games take us back to when we were children. We laugh, kid each other, and just are plain silly. But, others take a more serious route pushing us to search our relationship and ourselves to find that place where we can both grow in union and as individuals. Some require time together, while others, time alone. What works for us, what feels right for us, is the path we should endeavor to take. Harm to no one, honor and respect your mate at all times.

Good friends add to our delight in life. I cherish my friends so much. They are my teachers, and they seem to love me no matter what. Linda, my best friend, takes pleasure in watching Tom and I together. As a psychotherapist, she doesn't often see this sort of silliness in couples and apparently gets a kick out of watching us together.

A great many of us have forgotten what it's like to play in a relationship. It's a very necessary and important ingredient, but because of life's unavoidable stresses and busy schedules, often it's another of those essentials to get tossed aside.

Laughter and play are indispensable elements to balancing out the more serious and mundane aspects of life. Our body's react to laughter and childlike play with a great deal of enthusiasm both physically and emotionally. They allow us to vent and release the heaviness we hold so often within us. We're meant to laugh, play and enjoy the bounties of our lives. Fun is contagious and necessary for good health!

While my husband was attending the Naval War College in Newport we got to experience a full blown Nor'easter. While bathing leisurely in a lovely hot tub one evening after work, Tom snuck into the loo and dumped an entire snow shovel full of snow on top of my head..... No worries—he's been paying for it for the last twelve years. I wasn't all that upset, just a bit chilly. But then I suppose I do have an odd sense of humor, or at least that's what I've been told.

I love to dance, although I'm not very good at it. But in the confines of the cabin, who cares? Sometimes I turn on the music and just let my body get lost in it. I have a drumming CD one of our friends suggested I get. It's a great workout. Dancing brings a smile to my face, and to Tom's, if he happens to catch the act. I can't get him to join in for anything, so I just reserve that CD for my own space and time.

Humor is pretty subjective, and often one person's idea of something funny holds absolutely no humor whatsoever to another. When Tom and I started to date—in fact, on our second date—he helped me lug a huge planter full of dirt down the stairs of my house. At the bottom of the steps, my hand slipped, and down the planter came on my foot. In horror, he gasped and held his breath, waiting for my response. I started turning clammy and shocky, and he had to help me to the couch, but the whole idea of it started me in hysterics…go figure!

I guess we can choose laughter over a myriad of other responses. We can look at some things with humor and good grace, or we can choose to be angry and mean-tempered. Humor should never ever be used to shame or humiliate anyone. Using laughter as a tool against another is degrading and cruel.

I love tubs. Tom has little interest in them; nevertheless, he is gracious in defeat at darts or whatever other game we have attached a consequence to and hops right in if my prize is a bubble bath together. I do try hard to make it as appealing as possible. I place candles strategically about the bathroom, careful not to stick one under the window drape and set the curtains ablaze. I scented the tub, but not with anything too obnoxiously smelly, and have Buffett, his favorite, playing on the stereo in the living room. You can hear if from the tub. That's the hook. Relationships need a hook sometimes.

I've always thought a hot tub to be the perfect marriage counseling device. Of course a hot tub is too pricey for almost everyone, but it's such a good therapy tool: a glass of wine, good music, and who's going to run away from that one? No bother; right now, for us, a tub is almost as good.

Water creates a mood in which we find ourselves swept away into conversation until there is no more hot water left or we are pruned beyond recognition. We are both pretty small, so tubs work, and usually he's the one who ends up enjoying it more. I'm usually stuck at the faucet end of the tub (yes, another compromise), struggling to remain warm and bruise-free. It doesn't matter; I still cherish the time together. We usually don't have a ton of energy afterwards, but feel thoroughly relaxed and connected. We've learned not to have too many expectations and flow with the enjoyment of the moment.

Tom has started a tub and chicken tradition for when I get back from a visit with the kids. I have to take a train that comes into Sandpoint at the ungodly hour of 2:46 a.m. (not that I'm complaining; at least there's a train). I'm usually not really perky at that time of day, but he always has a delightful, bubbly bath waiting to relax and welcome me. Who wouldn't want to come home to that? He also has a chicken, all cooked and ready to eat. After a few nibbles, it's our dinner for the following evening.

We should feel protected and confident enough within our relationships and ourselves to try new and unique ways in which to have enchanting and memorable times with our most precious mate.

> *In embracing unconditional love you surrender all*
> *emotions and thoughts that separate you from well being harmony.*
> *This is the essential commitment in*
> *transformation and it must be renewed every day.*
> *Love is a daily celebration of aliveness and permission to go deeper.*
> – RICHARD MOSS, MD

Don't just do these sorts of things when you're in a good space. Try it when there's a bit of tension in the air; it tends to break down walls and allow for the start of good conversation.

Since our home is so small, we really have nowhere to go when we're upset with one another. We're forced to communicate. Like it or not, we talk it through as soon as we can stand it, unless someone is willing to sit and scowl in the barn again. I think we both have learned to deal more quickly with frustrations and irritations as they come up. It's obviously better to clear the air before things get really miserable.

Since we live where we do, it's a bit of a trek into town. It's a forty-minute drive over muddy, snowy, or dusty roads. My expectation for roads has gone from expecting them to be paved to settling for somewhat graded dirt. Consequently, there is mud, mud, mud everywhere in the spring. The snow can get pretty deep here too.

In the summer months, the land gives us plenty to do, but come winter, when the dark of the season confines us in our home, we find adopting somewhat of an agenda relieves some boredom and keeps our minds from turning to complete mush.

Most days books are good. Sewing, knitting, and spinning projects need work, or there's the occasional good movie to watch. Sometimes one of the kids deigns to call us and we get lost for hours in the news of their lives.

It can be tough alone in the cabin at times. It certainly tends to make one have to examine oneself and imagine how in the world those pioneers managed to stay sane. Tom spent the entire first winter here taping most of *Northern Exposure*, all eighty-odd episodes! So it was a process to find out how to survive here.

Tom loves to win things, so sometimes, as I think I might have mentioned, the prize for winning a game of cribbage might be a ten-minute back rub. Often we play a series of games, and the first one to win twenty-one games, for instance, wins an entire day! Some may think it's pretty pathetic to have to win something romantic or fun, but it's fun and helps keep things light. It really does turn out to be fun for all, except when I'm on a winning spree…funny how that doesn't go over well.

Much to the horror and embarrassment of our kids, we have brought the dartboard into the cabin. It hangs on the bathroom door at the end of the hallway.

I think they secretly think our relationship is sweet. I know they don't like the "visual" as they say, and I often tell them too much info, but I get more than my fair share from them too!

Many people attend church. We opt instead for the sanctuary of the woods. We offer thanks and share our gratitude for all who help and guide us through this world.

When the weather permits, we both like to hike into the back woods for a bit of time alone, but we do have to be constantly vigilant for the wildlife here, so deep meditation doesn't usually work for me.

Once in a while, give the gift of a day to your sweetie. Allow your partner to choose an adventure for both of you to enjoy together. Whatever he or she feels like doing—even if it sounds horrifying to you, do it anyway. Try to remain reasonable. Unless you're both up for bungee jumping off a cliff, don't do it! But with a winning attitude and some common sense, your day will most likely turn out wonderfully. Not only will you have a great adventure, your mate will also remember that you gave him or her a special treat, and feel especially loved and cherished. Remember to reciprocate. Goodness rebounds.

Although I enjoy Super Bowl Sunday to some degree, we all know I enjoy a day at the spa immeasurably more. So, we've made a deal. That particular Sunday is Tom's Day. This means I'm at his beck and call for the day. Whatever he wants, he gets. As I recall, the last one wasn't too painful, just some great sex and chips.

However, Valentine's Day is mine..ALL mine! Last time, I had another complete "spa day". I mixed up a batch of good old-fashioned oatmeal facial mush and got out some old forgotten nail polish, which I found this time. He painted my toenails a luscious rose color and gave me a great exfoliating facial. We have pictures to prove it somewhere too! He never said a negative word either. I also had a great bubble bath and an incredible massage. Super Bowl Sunday was a great trade-off!

For years and years, the egg hunts we devised at Easter time were for the kids, but I used to love making the eggs, hiding them and fixing the baskets. The best times were when it wasn't raining and we could hide the eggs in the backyard. I was probably more upset than the kids when they finally got too big for such things.

So we've chosen to make some changes of our own regarding egg hunts. When our kids come to visit, they look at us with a mixture of disbelief and envy, and probably some measure of embarrassment. We've traded in our old eyes for a new set. We do lots more laughing, hugging, strolling down the lane, and wishing on stars than we ever did before. We can see the magick and beauty in the smallest bud now, when before we just might not have noticed.

When the seasons roll around, we enjoy thinking up new events. Last Easter we had our own egg hunt; we bought colorful plastic eggs and filled them with all sorts of goodies. Some had candy; others had little pieces of paper with interesting, sexy, and challenging requests.

We are careful to put time limits on what we ask for. It makes for bad feelings to just demand that your mate drop everything to fulfill an Easter wish. Make sure you are both OK with the game's rules too. Last Christmas we found a stray egg under the sink. That was fun!

Playing games is just another way to have fun and connect on another level. Any little offering you attach to your favorite game just adds a bit of a twist to perhaps a worn-out game of Sorry or Monopoly.

So these little things we do that are silly and seem to some a waste of time can often leave us laughing at ourselves and each other in a way that only adds to what we think is a most important part of marriage—fun!

None of us is perfect. Humankind isn't meant to be. If you have created for yourself the life you have always thought possible, then by all means give yourself the time to relax into it. If you have made a bad choice along the way, then you need to ask yourself what it would take to make a change. Nothing can change if you don't begin the process.

Last summer after a trip into town, I arrived home to find a note attached to the front door. Tom was nowhere in sight. The note read, "Go to the well and look around." When I got there, I found another note directing me in another direction. If you think this sounds silly and childish, you're right! I was on a scavenger hunt for my husband! Being playful is a wonderfully freeing experience. It allows for all kinds of interesting new feelings to emerge.

To be creative is to be fresh and alive. To greet each new experience with an open mind and heart allows you to constantly surprise yourself and refresh your glorious partnership. It says you're special, and I want to help create for you and for us a most amazing life.

Balance

To learn to love and accept each other for the beautiful souls that we are seems to be a daunting task for most of us. As a couple, look at each other and see the glorious person before you. Loving yourself, loving your mate, and loving the people who surround your life are the first and best steps to being a spiritual person. We are here to learn to love.

Sadly, this is all a monumental task. Unconditional love is, to the majority of us, as remote and incomprehensible a subject as asking us to understand the universe itself. But it is nonetheless what humankind must touch to feel the wholeness of who we truly are or who we are capable of becoming.

Incorporating in our relationships what we as individuals and couples believe are our spiritual paths is not only an essential ingredient in our relationship, but one that tends to help carry on a sense of purpose for us. If we believe in a source that created and sustains us all, why not create a space in which to give thanks? Faith in a higher source can help hold us all closely together when times are desperate and the darkness of the soul looms ever so close.

This life of solitude and isolation we have chosen would be hopelessly out of balance for many folks. For us, there is an amazing spiritual component to life here in the woods. The simple tasks of gathering wood and tending the gardens have, for us, powerful consequences.

One of the most difficult objectives to incorporate into our lives is balance. We so often seem to think that balance is a fifty-fifty proposition. When we envision a seesaw in balance, we see it hovering in the air with both participants dangling equally. Balance is all too often seen as moderation, but balances can also encompass extremes.

There will be days when the scale is tipped way to one side. One person may have to carry the load if the other just can't manage for some reason. At another time, the other may have to step up to the plate. Define what balance means to you and your partner.

Most of the time, Tom and I have managed a good balance; he and I have divvied up the chores equally and are pretty happy with how things are working out between us. I just have to find that balance in other parts of my life. I could stand a bit of chaos in my life about now. Living out here is tough going. There can be too much quiet at times. So the gift of this lifestyle is a double-edged sword. At times, the seesaw is swinging all over the place.

Meditation is a good way to ground and center ourselves. It allows us that reconnection to Spirit many of us need so desperately. Some of us have lost the ability to be with ourselves, to sit silently and feel our hearts beat and hear our breath fill our lungs. Connection with that sacred part of us may help us recover that sense of self that we may have misplaced or neglected with our busy lives.

I have a difficult time clearing my mind of mostly everything. One thing that seems to work for me is to think of myself as radiating love out to the universe. I picture myself as a beacon and let myself just shine. We can all do this. This gives my mind something to do and seems to filter out the things that start eating at me.

There are many types of meditation. I took a seminar once that offered a walking mediation, and I fully enjoyed it. Essentially, we went outside and, silently but with great intent, walked barefoot, step by step into the grass. We were told to feel each blade of grass under our feet, to smell the spring air and drift away into our own minds.

Other times, sitting in a quiet space is lovely. Guided imagery is amazing too. This is where we generally listen to someone describing a place that we can envision. They may be describing a walk on the beach, where we can see and smell the saltwater and hear the gulls crying. They may be describing the leaves on an autumn day as they fall gently to the ground…but we are shown a vision and we try to be inside of it. It takes a bit of work to get to a place where you can actually feel free enough to experience this sort of thing, but keep working, because it is most certainly possible.

I think one of my favorite mediations is to go to my own sacred spot. This is a place that only I know about. It is a place that I have chosen and no one else can go to. If you love the beach or the woods, perhaps find a place in your imagination where you can find a cozy place to sit. It can be anywhere you want. A place you remember being as a child. Somewhere that brings you peace. It is there that in your meditation perhaps you will see people that have passed, or spirits of your guardians and those beings that help you in this life. You will be surprised who you will meet there. Open your mind and your heart. Ask them questions, tell them all about your life, allow this time to let go of this world and connect to all there is. There is so much more to this life than we think there is. Believe what you hear and what you see. Don't just dismiss your thoughts, but embrace them and think about what they mean in your life.

Find a quiet comfortable place to meditate. If you can sit upright, you might find you will actually stay awake for this. I topple over many times in the morning because I get so relaxed, I just can't always stay awake. I have a wonderful zafu and zabuton (yoga) pillows that I can sit on without getting all cramped up. Leg circulation can be a problem as we age, so it is important to be comfortable and let that blood flow. When I am ready, I burn my sage (a lovely Native American ritual that helps to clean and protect your sacred mediation area) and bless and protect my space, say my affirmations and prayers, and start deep-breathing exercises. When I finally settle into it, I find mediation profoundly moving.

Relationships run into problems easily because there is just so much to be on top of. I think balance smooths it all out. Too much of any one thing just doesn't seem work, no matter how wonderful it is. We have to know when to lead and when to let go.

The Last Little Bit

Our life here together on Snowhawk is continuing as it should. Our little cabin has since grown a bit larger with the addition of another few rooms, including another bathroom (thank goodness). We found that although Tom and I did very well together in such a small place, our kids got stuck out in the barn when they came for a visit. No one wanted to sleep in a tent! So we added a bit onto the existing cabin. We actually love it.

We have lost our wonderful George to the wilds of the woods and we miss him terribly. But, Tom bought home a wee little kitten we have since named Weasley. He weighs in now at twenty-one pounds of pure love.

Little Petie, our new Shih Tzu-Yorky puppy, is our delight as well, and has blended in with our other dogs beautifully. He gives us endless chuckles just looking into those big brown eyes and seeing his happy expressions of joy as he sits on the side of the pond and watches for the turtles to show up or a fish to jump. He is the only dog we have ever had that just seems to enjoy looking at things.

Living here has been such a wonderful experience for both Tom and I. Our relationship has had its up and own, as all do, but all in all we continue to be strong together.

Snowhawk is our refuge. She is our sanctuary where we can find the stillness we need to reconnect to each other and to this wonderful world. Not too many people have moved this far up the road yet, so we consider ourselves fortunate that we still have, except for the hum of a generator or two, lovely quiet and lots of solitude.

There are definitely those times when I long to be closer to my friends and family and wonder how we're ever going to get through another planting and harvest without having a coronary, but we manage. In the dead of winter I still get grumpy about the ice and snow and start looking at real estate, but so far I usually calm down come spring.

Tom decided that he wanted to fulfill a dream of teaching, and so after going back to school yet again for his certificate, he is teaching at the local high school. I went back to work while he was in school and for a couple of years after that, but mainly have been staying home, literally keeping the fires burning.

Still, in the fall there is plenty of wood to be chopped and hauled and equipment to be stored or fussed with, but come winter, Tom comes home to a warm house with good smells, and most days my heart is open to hearing about his day. It has been a blessing to live here, and we have both enjoyed this journey.

Whether we continue on this challenging path is up in the air—every bit of which is the way it should be. Indeed, there is a plan for each of us and growing to be done. We are having this incredible experience. It is unique to say the least. Every day we feel such gratitude for this life choice, even though it comes with many tradeoffs.

We may yet have another adventure left to us. If it is a choice we have, then we will look forward to it. If it is one of those curveballs, then we have each other to hold tight to.

Larry, our beloved and temperamental goose, is waddling across the lawn, ready to take on poor Marley. He has taken a distinct dislike to the poor boy. Marley emanates fear, and I think Larry must pick up on those vibes. Petie, the littlest and, it seems, boldest of all the dogs, hasn't yet incurred Larry's wrath. Because he doesn't exude fear, it seems he is able to run Larry back to his coop or into the pond.

It is quite a cute dance to watch as Petie slowly follows Larry to the pond. The lure of that big white bottom full of feathers just can't be denied. Larry often turns around to check out where he is, at which point Petie turns around and looks behind him too, so that perhaps

Larry won't notice him on his tail. This goes on again and again, until Larry finally gets to the pond's edge, at which point Petie usually pounces on him and grabs a mouthful of lovely down feathers right before the fateful plunge. It's all a delightful game to watch, but we are careful indeed to see no one gets hurt.

Animals have so much to teach us. They seem to take life as it comes. They give fully of themselves while living exactly in the moment..now that is something I strive for!

I try daily to match my intent to my actions. I try to be kind; I try to be considerate and compassionate. And of course, there are always those times when I fail. But it's the trying again and again that ultimately makes us who we are. We all know it's hard to fall, but hardest to pick ourselves up and march on again…and again. I wish it wasn't like this, but it makes us the people we are.

I believe we are all at different levels of soul growth. Some of us will, therefore, see and understand life's follies in ways other can't yet understand. Some of us find ourselves in circumstances that are unpleasant, while others seem to all the world as though they are carefree and unburdened. Many of our situations have been molded by our choices, but no matter what, no one is better or worse than another. We are all in this together, all cut from the same cloth, all one family.

Here in the woods, the balance of things is thrown in our faces daily. Everything needs to work together to work smoothly and, ironically, independently. Everything gives and everything receives.

It is a quiet life here at Snowhawk. Often I find that I must defend our choice to live here, although lately it seems we are more envied than not. We still don't have all the conveniences that make life easier. My son and daughter can't work from our cabin because we can't get cable out here yet. The roads are still hideous in the spring and winter. People find it too hard to get here in the winter months. But all in all, we have it better than most, and we have learned such a great deal about nature, about our relationship, and about ourselves that it has all been worth the effort to live this simple, gentle lifestyle.

The Christmas season is once again upon us. Much to Tom's horror, I put up that scrappy little artificial tree in the main room of the cabin again. Tomorrow I will once again gather the branches that will adorn our front door, and then, let the holidays begin!

It is another year of thanksgiving. To our children, our grandchildren, and everyone else we touch as we go along this road: good blessings, good cheer, and may your lives be full with the knowledge of your perfect being.